INTRODUCTION

My purpose in writing this book is to enlighten anyone who yearns to open their own resale store. This book is not only for those new to consignment but also for the many seasoned professionals I've had the pleasure to meet. Our shops bear many similarities, no matter what the contents of our resale inventories may be. My hope is to offer encouragement to those of you who are feeling at odds with the consignment gods.

As with any profession, there are days in which we doubt our path. After being in the business of resale since the year 2000 I have ridden the rollercoaster of emotions, but I'm extremely grateful that I stayed the course. Recently I had a horrible day, which led me to venting to my good friend Miranda Couse, a fellow entrepreneur. She listened attentively as I ranted about all that was bothering me. After a bit she suggested, "Close your shop and find another profession." It was such a matter-of-fact statement that it shocked me out of my stupor. Miranda knows me better than most people, and she knew that I needed a swift kick in the backside at that moment to shake me out of my pity party. My heart actually hurt at the thought of ever closing my doors. In that instant I realized that I needed to buck up and persevere.

My entire life led me to this industry and all that I have built. We are all human and life has its bumps, some of which are larger than others. There isn't a career path or business that is without great demands and difficult times. My hope is that this book brings you some peace of mind that you are not alone. I also hope that revealing my greatest disasters and learning moments will help you deal with yours along the way.

CONSIGNMENT FROM HOME

A Step-by-Step Guide Written from
Two Decades in the Retail Trenches

Kirsty Roefs

PART 1
BEGINNINGS

4

CHAPTER 1
OTHER PEOPLE'S THINGS

To understand my store and all the resale knowledge I gained from it, it's important that I take you back in time to one of my earliest memories. After all, our experiences are what mold us.

Ever since I can remember, I've loved looking through people's things. My grandparents owned an old farmhouse and it was packed to the rafters with over 40 years' worth of accumulation. My sister and I would love to play dress up with all the clothes, shoes and especially the costume jewelry. When my cousins would come to visit we would put on shows and make home movies using all the props and paraphernalia we could find. My grandmother would let us raid her closets and use whatever we found. Looking back, I don't know what in the world she was thinking, even though she would always bellow, "Just make sure you put it all back!" It never got put back.

Every kid growing up should have cousins. Cousins are amazing relatives to have and are so important while learning to adapt to adulthood. Some of my fondest memories are of my sister and me hanging out with my cousins, which consisted of playing, fighting, playing, fighting, repeat. One of my earliest business opportunities took place on our annual family camping trip at a nearby state park.

My cousin Jenny and I planned on making big money that summer. We saved our money and stocked up on penny candy from our local grocery store. Where we camped, on the top of a hill, there were no concessions stands. We smuggled our candy loot in along with our camping gear, dollar signs in our eyes. Our first store hours were a hit and we successfully sold our measly inventory at an insanely inflated price. With several pieces of candy still in stock, we couldn't wait to expand sales to the other kids at the campground.

My mother is many things, but a businesswoman is not one. When she learned of our candy business she immediately issued a cease and desist order. No amount of explanation would get her to change her mind. In one swift motion she put us out of business. Even though I explained the larger picture of exploiting the other campers, she was having none of it. Not only did we have to issue a full refund to my cousins and my little sister, but they had already devoured the merchandise! How unjust! Even my initial investment was gone.

It kept me up at night.

Another year I sent away for a catalog so that I could sell wrapping paper. The problem was that I lived on a dairy farm in the middle of nowhere. My poor neighbors! They must have cringed every time they saw me pedaling my banana seat bicycle up their driveways.

Just as important as our experiences and knowledge is our support system. My life has been enriched by my husband George. His support from the very beginning gave me the confidence to grow my dream to all that it is today.

My dream started in the home, hence the title of my first book "Consignment from Home!" the first much shorter version of which I wrote back in 2002. George helped me create a space in our home to accommodate consignors dropping off items for me to list on eBay. From there my vision grew and flourished. By working from home I was able to test the buying patterns of locals as well as consumers from all over the world. It also afforded me the opportunity to distinguish what was worth listing online and what had little to no resale value.

Some of my current consignors came from those first days. What better way to do research without a high cost of doing business? With a lot of hard work and determination, I now own a large brick and mortar store, which is thriving on a picturesque village main street. All things are possible and it is my hope that this book gives you the encouragement to pursue a career in this wonderful world of resale. To all of you reading this who are already in this industry, may this book give you the encouragement to stay the course and reach your full potential.

CHAPTER 2

MY FIRST SUPERHERO WAS A
JANITOR

Growing up poor is something that you either understand or you don't. While we had a roof over our heads and food in our bellies, there are certain things that define your childhood. Christmas, in particular, was extremely trying. All the kids in my class would write letters to Santa and ask for all sorts of toys and luxuries. Writing my list always gave me such hope. I would spend weeks honing my Christmas list from the toy book that would come in the mail. Then Christmas Day came and my list never bore fruit. Nevertheless, it was all still exciting and magical until I returned to school from Christmas vacation. All the other students would be boasting how Santa brought them expensive gifts. I berated myself, wondering what I had done to incur the wrath of Santa. Sure, new socks and a few toys were swell but why didn't he bring me that Cabbage Patch doll I so desperately wanted? This is very trying on a poor kid and let's face it, self-esteem is hard enough to come by without adding this stressor.

So Santa was never a huge hero in my world. There was, however, a man who did assume that role and he probably never even knew it. His name was Mr. R and he was a janitor with a heart of gold. He was from the bustling metropolis of New Jersey and had a summer home near our family farm. Whatever drove him to move to upstate New York is still a mystery to me. It is the closest thing to divine intervention that I will ever encounter.

The first time I met Mr. R was on a hot summer day in the early 80s. One of my favorite pastimes back then was to take my five Matchbox cars and make roads in the dirt. This entertained my little sister and me for hours. Our imaginations would take us to all sorts of destinations on those dirt roads. One day, we were outside playing when a wood paneled station wagon came rolling up. Not only was the wood paneling a showstopper, but so was the amount of smoke billowing out the driver's side window, as the man was smoking a sizable cigar. Our lives would be forever changed from that moment forward.

As Mr. R introduced himself to our family and built his summer home, he would become the most excitement we would see all summer long. It didn't take long until he, I'm assuming, realized that we were poor and in need of assistance. My parents were proud poor, which means that they would never accept a hand out. Mr. R was a smooth operator though and spun it to my parents that they would be doing him a favor if we would take the clean outs from the school where he worked as a janitor and find good use for them. That man will never know how much he redefined my life by this act of kindness.

The first load of black trash bags was something I will never forget. Bag after bag of discarded and forgotten clothing and shoes came to us. It was magical. These items were name brand and I couldn't believe that someone had let them go! One of the first batches was how I got my first pair of Nike sneakers. Back in the 1980s even I recognized the value and stature of owning a pair of Nike sneakers. They were two sizes too big and smelled. This didn't even faze me in my state of euphoria. Stuffing the toes with newspaper and scrubbing them was a small price to pay for the fact that I was now the proud owner of my first pair of Nike sneakers.

The bags continued to roll in and soon I was more excited to open those black trash bags than I was for the arrival of Santa. Mr. R never disappointed. It got to the point where I was arranging the bag contents in my grandfather's garage. Without even realizing it, I was learning the art of display and merchandising. Mr. R had given me the best gift of all when he introduced me to those bags. Not only did I recognize the value in discarded objects, but I was given the gift of the entrepreneurial spirit. He will never know how instrumental he was in my upbringing. All because he had a kind heart and good intentions. More people could benefit from his way of thinking.

Mr. R shaped my life without his even knowing it. There are no regrets when I look back on my childhood. The kindness I was shown and the compassion of others has formed me into the businesswoman I am today. It is my mission to show others compassion. This takes many different shapes in my life. It's announcing an impromptu "sale" that benefits a struggling mother and allows her to buy both the necessary item as well as the splurge purchase. It's allowing a forlorn grandmother who was just granted full custody of her grandchildren to be able to outfit them for school. To this day I still get heart palpitations when I go through people's things. (Let me clarify that I'm referring to the items they bring in to consign. I'm not sneaking into their homes in the dead of night to rifle through their belongings.)

CHAPTER 3
SELLING THE SHIRT OFF MY BACK

The Spanish language has always fascinated me. Combine that and a thirst for travel and you get me working after school at an insurance agency and babysitting in all my free time to save for an exchange program trip to Spain. It took every cent I had to pay for the trip and when the time came for the actual experience, I had under $200 to spend on the trip. Living in Barcelona on $200 a month is less than ideal.

My wardrobe consisted of Mr. R clothing, and after 10 years of sorting his trash bags, I had learned which brands were sought after. Not gonna lie; I had super cool outfits. Levi's and rock and roll T-shirts, Nike high tops, Puma sneakers, I had them all and they were all used. Keep in mind that this was 1990 and the internet was not a thing yet. Europeans did not have ready access to our American brands. All those teenagers wanted the American brands and most didn't even know how to get their hands on them. So in Spain I became a walking billboard and was selling all of my used clothes for a tidy profit. This was my first real experience with resale. Totally unaware, I had taken my first step on the resale road.

CHAPTER 4
THE COLLEGE YEARS

All these crazy antics and adventures never dimmed my desire to try and run my own business. Somewhere along the way though, I lost sight of my dreams while growing up. Bound and determined to see the world and go to college, I strayed from my entrepreneurial spirit. The safety and security of a teaching career was calling my name. Upon returning to the States and entering college, I would continue picking through piles of clothing at yard sales. After laundering these scores I would consign them in the local consignment shop. This helped me pay for many textbooks during the lean college years. Again, all these experiences helped mold my resale knowledge. Without even understanding it, I was working on a much grander plan for my life.

While attending college, scouring weekend estate sales and thrift stores for items to clean up and consign, I became what is known as a picker. It wasn't until I discovered the book *Too Good to be Threw* by Kate Holmes, and started following her blog, that I realized I was not the only one. Not only was I intrigued by repurposing items, but I loved the idea of channeling my energies to provide a more upscale feel to this style of shopping. As I stood in line to drop off items for consignment I would find myself mentally rearranging the store. One of my favorite things to do was arrange the miscellaneous wares into a display. The owner, Cheryl, would place things out on metal shelving she got from a grocery store that had gone out of business. The sterile look drove me nuts and I would pretend to shop while rearranging the shelves into displays. Without a doubt, I was probably a giant pain in the neck to that poor owner.

One particular weekend during my senior year of college, it hit me that my heart lay in consignment and resale. My conversations with Cheryl began to change. She was very candid in her answers and I wish I was still in touch with her. Some of the concerns or frustrations she had shared with me, now make complete sense. At the time I thought she might be a bit too high strung or exaggerating her situation. Just for thinking that, I owe her an apology. This business is demanding and not for the faint of heart. It takes true dedication and a love for resale to create an atmosphere in which people truly connect with you and want to do business with you. If you think you will be able to enjoy a life of leisure, coming and going as you please, you need to look elsewhere. Even after getting an inkling of all it would entail, I was prepared to go forward and embark on a career in consignment.

At the time, I was engaged to someone to whom I felt compelled to tell my consignment plans. His look of horror at the prospect of a consignment shop is probably what did in our relationship. When someone feels so passionately about a dream, it is not for others to crush that spirit simply because they can't imagine the work or possibilities. It was an eye-opening experience and one of several reasons why we broke off the engagement and I moved back to my hometown.

CHAPTER 5
WINNING THE LOTTERY

Have you ever heard of the old expression, when one door closes, another opens? That is exactly what happened. Upon moving home it became clear that living with my parents was not a feasible option for several reasons. As an adult it's difficult to go back to living under your parents' roof and living by their rules. This led me to eventually apply for a live-in nanny position in my hometown. When I saw the ad in the paper, I couldn't believe it. It was the ideal situation. Free room and board plus a living stipend for just babysitting!? This would allow me to continue my educational career and finish my studies. Life was looking up every day.

The day of the interview came, and I discovered that the man in need of a nanny was recently separated and had two small boys in need of a full time caregiver. At least I think that's what he said. When he answered the door and I realized it was the good-looking mechanic, George, who owned a nearby automobile repair shop, I was ready to work for free. Throw into the mix an adorable six-month old and an inquisitive two-year old and my career path was forever altered.

Now before anyone gets twisted about my change of plans, I need to say that I did make a valiant attempt to juggle school and children. The insane idea of an easy babysitting gig was quickly shot as I realized that there were very real responsibilities. A poopy diaper waits for no student. The older boy, Tristin, had an endless stream of questions. It was often a concern of mine that my ears might actually start to bleed from the incessant chatter and questioning. The baby, Bryden, was a serious mischief magnet. He was crawling before I even thought it was humanly possible. I went from being a happy go lucky, partying college student one weekend, to quite literally a mother figure to two small children the next. Life was a joy even while scrubbing the poop mural off Bryden's crib slats. Schooling was proving more difficult amidst the rigors of keeping up with two small yet mighty boys.

My sign came one afternoon as I was struggling to write out an essay that was due that evening. After feeding Bryden a bottle and holding him in one arm, I attempted to finish up the four-page essay. Oblivious to the fact that I forgot to burp that poor baby, my concentration was broken as he proceeded to spit up all over my arm, pen and essay paper. To this day I'm not sure what prompted me to start laughing. Maybe it was hysteria however the laughter kept coming and soon baby Bryden was giggling too. We couldn't stop laughing. His spit up was dripping down his chin and it was the funniest moment of awakening. There was no more schooling in my future until these boys were older. They needed me and my heart wasn't in the schooling. My heart was with them and seeing to their needs. While I felt relief over having made a decision, Tristin toddled over to demand why we were laughing. Life was good.

Setting forth on my nanny years, without even realizing what I was doing, I had returned to resale. With the boys, we would set out to shop various sales and sell through local consignment shops. We even grew to having an antique booth at a local vendor market. The added money was nice and it made me start to realize what housewares were selling and which were not. Without even knowing, I was researching what drove the local market.

As my relationship evolved with this man and his children, we would spend hours sharing our life goals amidst the chaos of children. Our common ground of business led to several discussions about marketing, the economy and customer service. When I finally told him my dream of opening an upscale resale shop, he was not only supportive but he was a great sounding board and still is today.

After George and I were married it only became more clear that I loved the world of used goods. With small children and my husband as the sole breadwinner, money was tight. This was a small price to pay for the ability to stay home with our small children. We made do, and I became adept at searching for secondhand deals. It was always my favorite pastime but now it was a means of buying secondhand deals and re-marketing them to sell for a higher price. This not only helped occupy my mind (in a constant state of Legos and Sesame Street), but it gave me the extra money to spend on my home and family.

As the era of the internet emerged, an entirely new market became available. Combine this with my housebound life of motherhood and my resale experience went in a new direction. It was in the year 2000 that my first business was born and I began conducting consignment from home.

PART 2
CONSIGNMENT FROM HOME

ONLINE SALES

For the longest time I've had to educate people about the term consignment. My personal definition is that it's an arrangement between someone with items to sell (the consignor), and a businessperson who takes in those items to sell. The sale price is then split between the two. Different shops use different percentage splits. Most often those splits are either 50/50 or 60/40. There are some shops that even adopt a buyer's fee for each item. This additional, nominal fee is tacked on to the selling price of the item. It is not included in the consignment split as this fee is used to help offset the cost of doing business. Keeping the lights on and so forth.

With today's heavy presence of online sales sites, there is a targeted market for most anything. At the initial emergence of the internet, the only main site for online sales was eBay, and for a long time it dominated the market. Slowly, other successful sites have emerged, making it easier for people to list their items.

Most online sites charge fees for the listing of each item. Usually these fees are paid out of the initial sale amount. Another alternative for sellers is to pay the fees out of their cut of the sale price. It is imperative to determine how you would like to handle payment of listing fees. Make it clear up front and in writing with the consignor. You must keep in mind that items are usually entrusted to the care of the business until it is sold to the buyer. Once the item is sold, the consignment business pays the consignor. This process is very similar to the operation of a standard brick and mortar consignment store, however all inventory is listed online. When I say "online" I am referring to the many different online sales sites found on the internet.

Examples of these sites are:
eBay (ebay.com)
Tradesy (tradesy.com)
Instagram (instagram.com)
Poshmark (poshmark.com)
Letgo (letgo.com)
Craigslist (craigslist.org)
Facebook Marketplace (facebook.com)
Etsy (etsy.com)

The list continues to grow with new sites popping up all the time. You have the ability to determine which site suits the products you sell. That's just one of the many perks of having an online consignment business.

An online consignment sales service allows you to own and operate your own consignment shop without any of the expensive overhead and miscellaneous costs of a brick and mortar storefront. With the proper advertising and preparation, you will be able to manage a successful online consignment service right out of your own home and even in your spare time! With lots of hard work and strategic growth you should be able to grow your business as little or as much as you like.

Why an online consignment business? After all, nearly everyone has access to computers, smartphones, the internet and the many listing sites. They could all, in theory, list their own items and keep all the profit for themselves. What many people don't have, however, is the organization and the dedication to actually list their items, monitor their sales, ship promptly, and give great customer service. Many people know of the sites and how to list and have even posted a few items, or their exposure to the online sales trend might be only in the capacity of buying. Regardless, in the hurried world of today, many lack the time or energy to post all their items. Committing time to staying on top of listings and answering customer inquiries takes organization. This is where you market yourself and your online sales service as a benefit to them. Take the work out of the equation for them. Make it clear how it benefits them to take advantage of all you offer. These people are your main target market. Your online sales service is designed to assist them and make their life easier while making them money.

This section is designed to assist you in all aspects of owning and operating your own online consignment sales service. This type of business has very low startup costs. It is also the type of business that has limitless earning possibilities depending on how much effort you put forth. I am a firm believer in this business and feel that there is much opportunity online. By posting your consignors' items on the many different online sales sites, you will be giving them vastly more exposure than a consignment store shelf. Every day millions of people from around the world are looking for specific items on various auction sites. In addition, the entire world of social media is available to you. Social sharing is easy with such platforms as Facebook, Instagram, Twitter, Pinterest, Snapchat, Podcasts, YouTube, and more. These sites offer you the opportunity to reach a broad array of audiences. One thing to remember, though, is that it is virtually impossible to be an expert on all social platforms. My experience has taught me that it is better to do one or two platforms exceptionally well than to attempt a presence on several of them. Once you have dabbled in all of them and decided which suits your needs the best, you are ready to start utilizing them and making sales. What better way to obtain the highest price for that odd item that no longer serves a purpose to its owner than to know how to best market it?

There are several advantages to starting this type of business. As I said, low startup costs are number one. If you go the consignment route, your inventory is supplied at no charge. You have the option of having a small business or expanding to a larger business. Word of mouth spreads quickly especially when you are offering a service like this. It is very possible to gain a rapidly growing customer base in no time. This success will grow even faster once you prove yourself as a seller and your current customers share their positive experiences with their friends. Word of mouth is one of the most valuable advertising methods. If you conduct your business well and with integrity, your advertising will be practically free. Another advantage is that you can test the waters before you leap. You don't have to quit your day job in order to start this type of business.

The list of advantages of online consignment is lengthy. One feature is that you can work on your business any time of the day or night. Online auctions, listing sites and social media are open 24 hours a day, seven days a week. This flexibility allows you to work the online business around your busy daily schedule. If you are ambitious enough, it is entirely possible to continue outside employment as well as run a successful online consignment sales service. The choice is yours!

Despite all these advantages, there are a few things to remember. Some people love their "stuff" and honestly believe it is worth a small fortune. This can be a nuisance to deal with. Make sure you have your business contract prepared prior to beginning your business interactions. Also, clearly state your rules up front and in writing in order to avoid any conflict down the road. As you research your business, be sure to take notes regarding what policies and procedures you do and don't agree with. By looking at other businesses and determining what fulfills your vision, you are laying the foundation of your new business model.

CHAPTER 6
WHERE ARE ALL THE PEOPLE?

The first step is to establish contact with your prospective consignors. Start advertising and using word of mouth to produce a steady flow of contacts. Here is where you need to be prepared. For instance, where exactly do you want to conduct business with your consignors? Does your home have adequate space for an office in which to meet? If you do not have that option, consider either meeting your consignors at their homes or at a neutral location. Be sure to keep it safe, especially if you do not know the individual. Don't be afraid to have a friend tag along. You can always claim they are there to assist you in moving items. Quite possibly you will want to do both, meet at your office as well as make house calls. This is your business. You make the decision as to what is most convenient for you.

CHAPTER 7
FUNDING YOUR NEW VENTURE

Although consignment is one of the least expensive businesses to start, there are still some expenses. The more you can limit these, the better. You can always expand later, so it is better to not go broke initially trying to outdo yourself.

As I said, there are little to no costs in starting an online consignment sales service. Your essential investment will be your camera. Recent smart phones come with amazing cameras. Using one of these also allows you to load merchandise directly online without immediate need of a computer. The camera is the heart of your business. Your merchandise must be presented well, and your camera is your personal selling tool. Without pictures, you are not going to be making money

CHAPTER 8
WRITING YOUR BUSINESS PLAN

Writing a business plan is not for the faint of heart. It is, however, essential if you need to secure a business loan. But even if you don't need outside funding, I strongly recommend that you put together a business plan. It is not only beneficial in the financial sense, but also forces you to set down your vision of all that you wish your store to become. Writing a business plan affords you the opportunity to take into consideration all the important aspects of your business. It also guides you in researching your competition as well as costs of doing business in your particular area. These are all factors you should know in order to open a business with the greatest chance of success.

There are many reasons why a business plan is necessary. Not only can it be used to influence financial institutions to loan you money, but it forces you to work out the essentials of your business. A business plan guides you through the innermost workings of your model. This is an excellent opportunity to delve deeper and ensure future success.

The first step to this process is to clearly define your business by writing a **Company Description**. Your business's name and contact information only skims the top. A well-written business plan would include a summarized overview of how your business is going to fulfill a need. Its vision must be set forth. How is the prospective industry doing in your area? Why is it even a good idea to open up this sort of business? You will also need to demonstrate why you are a qualified candidate to start this type of business. The business competition you would be facing must be outlined. Research your competitors' weaknesses. Then explain how you will improve their shortcomings to make your business a success. Just as important is to research competitors who are a success. Break down the reasons why they are a success. How could you emulate their successful business model in your own way?

The second step is to tackle your **Marketing Plan**. You must thoroughly understand your target market in order to appeal to them. Who are the people who will be your consumers? You must break down how exactly you will reach them. Be sure to consider demographics, or WHO your target market is. What age group are they? What can they afford? What do they do for fun? Is your business a want or a need? What are their personal goals and how does YOUR product help them achieve that? Where do these people hang out? Are they online? Do they use email, Facebook, or are they old school and prefer newsprint? What advertising will you utilize? Once you have defined these factors, you have your ideal consumer.

Operational plans are complex, but it forces you to take a closer look at some of the mundane yet important procedures. You should be able to outline the entire business process. Who will provide you with your products to sell? What type of quality? What items do you need to start up? Tagging process, arrangements of various departments, customer service policies, what to do with expired merchandise, and the list goes on. This is the step to outline your processes from start to finish.

Lastly, a **Financial Analysis** needs to be written. Here is where you demonstrate what expenses you will expect. Creating a budget helps immensely as it makes you take into consideration and outline all the various expenses you will incur. Then you should be able to explain how you will generate revenue over time. If you plan on slowly implementing wholesale items to help subside slow times of the year, project that. Do you plan on having special blow out sales to help generate revenue at key dates throughout the year? These are all important elements to include.

That is the very basic outline for a business

plan. Before even attempting the business plan, it's important to reflect on yourself and fully know your why. When I say WHY I'm asking you to reflect on the real reason you want to go into business. What motivates you to rock this industry that you are about to embark on? Once you can define that, you let that be your guide. Whenever you are stuck on a decision, remember WHY you started your business. WHY you sacrificed certain things to give your business the opportunity to grow.

Does this sound like a boring proposition? Maybe, however, it's necessary for you to think out the particulars before jumping blindly off a cliff into entrepreneurship. Owning your own business can be so rewarding. At times. It can also be extremely stressful and downright discouraging at other times. Perseverance is easier when you have a clearly defined reason WHY. Helps you reflect on your original dream during adverse times when you catch a customer pooping in your storage closet. Yes, that really happened.

If you think writing a business plan is a one time thing, think again. As your business evolves, you will need to rework it from time to time. It's important to continually reassess your plan too! Don't think of a business plan as a dreaded task. Instead, consider it as a chance to grow your business. It's an excellent way to map out its future and give it direction. Where do you want to be in six months, one year, five years, etc. Dream goals should be realistic. Write them down. If you had told me 20 years ago that I would grow so large that I would have to move my family out of our original business site and into our own home so that House of Consignment could take over, I would have never believed you! The sky's the limit. Especially when you aren't afraid of hard work.

CHAPTER 9
ORGANIZATION OF ONLINE SALES:
GET IT TOGETHER

A handwritten log will work wonderfully with a small sized operation. If you are going to be handling hundreds of peoples' items and selling them online, I urge you to seriously consider a software program. This is a deductible cost of doing business that will save you much time and headache while also allowing you to spend more time on sales, which is what makes you money. Please refer to the section regarding software for more information pertaining to choosing a system that works for you.

While selling online and from home seems much simpler than running a brick and mortar store, it has its headaches as well. Once you begin listing you will be (with luck!) making sales. As the items sell, you must have a system in place that allows you to easily locate the sold item and get it shipped out to its new owner as quickly as possible. My business still sells online, and this is one of the biggest challenges we face. Having a system in place that allows you to speed up your process time is something that is unique to your business. We all have different space accommodations as well as organizational preferences.

The following are a few things to keep in mind when inventorying your items for safe keeping until they sell online:

Who consigned this item?

What date was it consigned?

Which selling site(s) is it listed on?

These are all important pieces to know so that you may better track an item's performance as well as monitor who needs to be paid.

CHAPTER 10
SETTING UP YOUR OFFICE SPACE:
WHERE DID I PUT THAT?

Setting up your office space is another important element in successfully operating your own home business. There is a lot of paperwork maintenance involved with this type of business. The better suited your office space is to handle your business, the less time you will have to spend searching. Your time needs to be devoted to selling items, which means making you money!

It is very easy to be overcome with STUFF! More than once I have begun my day with a clean desk only to get on a roll listing items and discover that I cannot even find my keyboard! Devise a system of organization to help you maintain order.

Once I left out an important pile of invoices that

needed to be reviewed for my sales tax filing. My daughter Gracie was around six years old and had just learned how to make snowflakes out of paper. After having stepped out into my shop for a mere five minutes, I returned to my entire stack of invoices cut up into beautiful snowflakes. It made for an interesting evening trying to put them back together again. The Christmas spirit was strong that year!

One final thought is to keep in mind that if your consignors are coming into your office space you need to project a professional image. Don't give them a reason to fear for their items when left in your care. You don't want to lose a potential consignor because they're afraid you'll lose their items amongst the stacks of merchandise piled around your desk.

CHAPTER 11
EMAIL CORRESPONDENCE:
MODERN DAY PONY EXPRESS

Inquisitive emails are sometimes frustrating when they come in floods. Once I listed a motorcycle helmet on eBay and forgot to mention the size in the description. At the time I didn't realize that I could add to my description after having started my auction. So for one week I received over 30 emails asking what size the helmet was. My responding emails started out being very jovial:

"Hello! Thank you for inquiring about the black motorcycle helmet on eBay. The size of helmet is large. If you have any further questions, please feel free to contact me. Thanks again, Kirsty."

After about the fifteenth email my responses

were quite different. They simply read, "large." I cannot stress to you enough how important your listing's title and description is for every single item. Your bidding prices depend on you alone. Having a well written auction title and description complete with great photos helps prospective buyers feel more confident in placing their bid. If a serious bidder is unclear on a size or color, etc., they will email you and ask. But what about the less persistent buyers? Maybe some possible bidders moved on rather than spending their online shopping time typing away to ask what should have already been listed. If you've listed an item and later realize (probably from a buyer's email) that you have left out a key point, look for an "edit items" link or tool so that you can go in and add the information to your listing right away.

Reading and rereading unimportant emails takes up your valuable time and can create confusion. Setting up your mail service with the proper folders will make you better able to meet the needs of your customers. For example, my email Inbox is set up with several folders. Before the emails are even organized and posted to various email folders they are kept in the Inbox. Emails are kept in the Inbox until I have properly responded to them. If your Inbox is clogged with useless emails, you can't sort out the important ones. That's why I always delete those emails from eBay that let me know I have listed an auction. My way of thinking is that all that information is already clearly detailed in the "My eBay" page. If you look under your selling page, it's all listed there. The emails in my Inbox are just duplicates, and all they do is take up unnecessary space. On the other hand, if I receive a notification that an item did not sell, I am sure to keep it. After all, I might want to post it again at a future time. So I set up a "Re-List" folder to put this type of email into. On a slow day I can simply click on the links provided in these emails and within a matter of minutes have the auction listed again. It's also easy to adjust the price while re-listing to help facilitate a sale.

CHAPTER 12
PACKAGING:
WITH A PRETTY BOW ON TOP

Once an item sells, it's time to seal the deal. If you have all the mailing necessities on hand, it will minimize the time spent packing the item for shipment. It's been my experience that the more I save on supplies, the more money I can invest in other areas of my business. Enlist your friends, neighbors, and relatives to help gather shipping supplies. Make them all aware that you are always looking for packing supplies. You would be surprised at how many households throw away the bubble wrap, tissue paper, and Styrofoam "popcorn" they receive in the mail. Lots of people buy online or through mail order catalogs, which generate these types of supplies. Most often people are delighted to save the packaging they accumulate. Be prompt when they ask you to pick up their pile. You don't want to irritate them by not picking up, or they might opt to discard these valuable packing supplies. Also, be sure to check the supplies to be sure they don't have any odors or stains. By recycling these costly mailing "accessories" you will be able to cut down on expenses and increase your profits!

Packaging your item for shipment to its new owner is not always as simple as throwing the item in a shipping envelope and dropping it off at your local post office. The new owner is still anticipating the item they have not yet seen in person. Presentation is essential at this point. Leave no room for uneasiness. Do a neat and tidy job in packaging your products. This will reassure your customers. With so many different online sources, make it your mission to stand out.

Let's talk about how it feels to receive a package in the mail. Personally, I still love to see a package arrive in my name. With all the different online shopping options, your packaging is another very distinct opportunity to make your business stand out from the mass. Let's discuss how to make that happen.

Go the extra mile by wrapping clothing items in tissue paper. We've upgraded to adorable "thank you" stickers, which hold the tissue paper in place. Make the presentation a true reflection of your store's brand. Do you have an attractive logo you can print up as a stamp or sticker to reinforce your branding? This piece of the sale is just as important as the photos, the listing, and everything else. You have a captivated consumer that you want to impress so that they become a routine shopper.

For shipping clothing and unbreakable items, a sealable plastic shipping bag has so many advantages. They keep your items dry and they do not open easily. If you search to find them to purchase in bulk, don't just jump at the first lot of plain white bags. There are so many interesting and fun prints of bags out there! It is my opinion that this is a way to snag your customers' attention and make them feel special. This is money well spent if it makes them pause to take in your beautiful presentation.

Be sure delicate items are packed properly so that when your customer picks up their package it doesn't clunk and bang around, making the customer fear potential damage. Your buyers' feedback will make or break your business. This point cannot be stressed enough.

Follow through with branding yourself by inserting a professional looking flyer or card with the contents of the package. Inserting your business information helps grow your customer base and encourages repeat business. This reinforces that you are a professional source for all their needs. Your information should include at a minimum your business name, and how to locate you on social media and various selling sites. If you have a website be sure to have that prominently displayed. Any business brick and mortar locations should be printed on the flyer as well. Think of this flyer as a tool to cross promote all your business platforms. With any luck, your customer will look you up and do repeat business with you or, better yet, send their friends your way because they are so impressed with their experience with you.

CHAPTER 13
WORD OF MOUTH ADVERTISING:
GO SHOUT IT FROM A MOUNTAIN

A prime source of advertising, and the most economical by far, is word of mouth. There are a variety of ways to better access this medium. Create business cards and flyers that clearly explain your business and how it works. It's best to have a detailed brochure that covers all the particulars of your business venture. A brochure is the best medium for disclosing your terms of service. Give extras of these to customers so they can pass them along to their friends, neighbors, relatives and co-workers. You would be surprised at the number of people who will be receptive to the idea of "turning their clutter into cash," especially when the business is recommended by someone they know.

Many office store chains offer a variety of business card packages. For the best return on your money, I would suggest using an online printing service such as www.vistaprint.com, which runs periodic sales and offers. As you start out, you'll want several brochures available at all times to pass out. Don't forget to give friends and relatives several so that they too may pass along your business information. Remember to carry them with you everywhere! You never know when you'll strike up a conversation with someone and wish you had a brochure to hand them.

CHAPTER 14
THE BIG MESSAGE:
MOTHER EARTH MAKES MY DAY

Remember that not only are you starting your own business, but you are helping the world recycle. Every day, countless useful items are thrown away simply because their owner has outgrown their need for them. This is unfortunate, especially considering that there are so many people without the means to purchase these same items brand new. Essentially, you are helping in the recycling process. Be sure to stress this added value to prospective customers and consignors.

CHAPTER 15
ACCEPTING CONSIGNMENTS:
IN THIS CASE,
SWEAT THE SMALL STUFF

Don't be too critical when it comes to the type of consignments you accept. By this I am not saying to sell something you personally feel is immoral or unethical. Just remember that "one man's trash is another man's treasure." Don't limit your possibilities by accepting only consignments that you deem attractive or interesting. Given the variety of people who purchase online, the chances of finding a potential buyer for just about anything is great. Keep an open mind when it comes to making online sales.

Be sure to inspect all incoming consignments. It's important to know what you are selling. Examine all items, carefully looking for rips, tears, missing pieces, stains, etc. Having fluorescent lighting overhead helps you find stains or blemishes. Don't bother putting your time and effort into listing something that won't sell.

There are a few things to remember, as is the case with any business. Many people honestly feel that their "stuff" is worth the big bucks. They are often wrong. Avoid any potential problems by addressing the value of your consignors' items right away. Make it very clear in the contract as well. Determine the consignor's bottom line price so you won't upset them later on. You don't want to sell Aunt Mabel's bedpan collection for a whopping $20 only to have Betty Sue have a fit because she assumed it would fetch a much higher price. If Betty Sue comes in with a bedpan collection, you might mention to her that they used to be in high demand, but the market has softened lately. Perhaps if she wants to make a killing on her bedpans, she might want to look at local auctions. Say you can't guarantee a firm result, but if she just wants to get rid of them, you are happy to list them for her.

CHAPTER 16
YOUR CONTRACT:
PLAYING BY YOUR RULES

When it comes time to prepare your contract, it's best to first list the key elements. Decide on your commission percentage. Decide on your policies and procedures. Even though a business plan is primarily used to obtain bank funding, it is beneficial to create one to use as an operating guide. This allows you to think through a variety of necessary business decisions prior to opening. As you do more business it is possible, even likely, that you will change your mind about certain policies. **Don't be afraid to make business changes based on experience that you have gained in the first stages of operation**. This is what being an entrepreneur is all about.

A sample contract from which you may draw ideas is on the following page.

Online Consignment Sales Service Contract

Business name, address and phone number

Below are the terms of our contract for consigning with [BUSINESS NAME]:

1. Items are to be clean, in good condition and marketable. [BUSINESS NAME] reserves the right to decline on any items they feel are not up to these standards.

2. [BUSINESS NAME] will use its best efforts to promote the sale of items for consignee.

3. You will receive _____ % of the final sale price of your consigned item.

4. Contract term is _____ days.

5. [BUSINESS NAME] shall use its best efforts to care for consigned property. However, the consignor leaves all items at his/her own risk. The consignee shall not be held responsible for the loss, destruction, or damage of consigned items.

6. If unsold items are not picked up at the conclusion of the contract period (___ days), then they will become the property of [BUSINESS NAME] to dispose of at their will.

7. A statement of account will be given to each consignor upon request.

I, _____, consign items for resale by [BUSINESS NAME] and agree to all of the terms stated above.

BUSINESS NAME   DATE

CONSIGNOR   DATE

Let's break down all the various components of a consignment contract. After all, there are some serious issues to decide on before you even open up for business.

What percentage do you want to split with the consignor?

What do you want to do with their unsold items?

How long do you want to give their items before you deem them unsaleable?

Remember that this manual consists of all the things to keep in mind while you are figuring out what business practices you want to follow. This business allows you to own and operate your own consignment shop without any of the expensive overhead. With the proper advertising and set up, there is no reason you can't run a successful online consignment shop right out of your own home!

PART 3
TAKING THE LEAP TO
BRICK & MORTAR

THE BIRTH OF THE HOUSE OF CONSIGNMENT

At the very heart of every business is its creator. You must never lose sight of the important role you play in your business's life. You are the voice and the biggest advocate for the success of your creation. When I first told people in 1996 that I wanted to open an upscale resale shop that felt more like a boutique than a used shop, people thought I had gone mad. My parents thought I was insane to give up on a teaching degree to chase a dream. This is where the entrepreneurial spirit separates us from most people. That said, I am not saying that this is all it takes. For years I planned, and I researched. To be honest, I would have never had the confidence to take the plunge had it not been for my husband George. He listened earnestly to my detailed ideas of all things consignment. Never did he mock me or belittle my ideas. With his help I wrote my first business plan in 1998. It was upon completion of that business plan that I realized that my current dream would fail. There needed to be more of a cushion if I was to sustain the business until it was able to pay for itself; that was the harsh reality. My initial thought was to say the hell with it and try anyway. However, I just couldn't bring myself to risk that approach and have my dream fail. Many tears were shed and then I pulled on my big girl panties and dug deeper.

In 1999, eBay had become the hottest ticket on the planet, yet not many knew how to use it, myself included. At this point I need to give credit to my cousin Nick who explained what eBay was and how to use it. His suggestion to try it was the soundest advice I'd ever been given. Battling with our first computer, which we financed through Gateway, and a horrible little digital camera, which took forever to import photos, I persevered and before I knew it I was listing and selling on eBay. Shopping with my young sons on the weekends allowed me to score items to list while also amassing an amazing inventory of Legos. It was one of the best times of my life.

An amazing thing happened the more I listed and sold online. People would hear about it and ask me how to do it. With my background in teaching I approached a local adult and continuing education school about offering a course on how to sell online. My gut was telling me that people would love to have the tools to sell for themselves. The administration jumped at the opportunity and soon I was teaching in the evenings to adults trying to understand the mysterious ways of the World Wide Web. My classes were well attended, which encouraged me. The biggest challenge was trying to talk them out of begging me to take their belongings and sell them online for them. Apparently, it was too much of an undertaking and they would rather consign their stuff with me and have me do the work. Afraid to get my hopes up, I accepted only a few people's items. Listing online while my boys were pretending to nap was becoming my life. Making a steady income while living my dream of being a stay at home mom was pure magic. The incoming piles of name brand wares and unique antiques never ceased. My dining room resembled a mailroom and my den was draped in various fabrics as backdrops and my trusty Gateway computer. Life was good.

While juggling motherhood and an emerging business it hit me to share my expertise in the form of a book. In my mind, the joy I experienced must speak to everyone. My first book, "Consignment from Home" was written in 2002. Having no guidance, I had it printed and bound and then marketed it on none other than eBay. The sales from this manual encouraged me to take on more consignors. Honestly, my original book was very simplistic and was indebted to my new awareness of emerging computer terms. In my mind, it was a groundbreaking book of significant technological value. In fact, what this book gave me was the courage to pursue my original dream of owning a brick and mortar consignment store.

After operating from home, it was becoming clear that there was a real need for a local brick and mortar store. While consignors were dropping off their wares for me to sell online, they were poking into the items others had dropped off. People wanted quality used housewares at an affordable price. My mind was working on overdrive as to how to make this happen.

Reworking my plan gave me hope. It made me rethink all the costs and expenses associated with owning a business. The years that I spent running "Consignment from Home" afforded me the chance to gain a better grasp of the industry.

While all of this was happening, our little family welcomed a tiny bundle of joy in the form of baby girl Jorja. She was named after her Dad and amidst a hormonal meltdown I had decided to make the spelling of her name unique. Life was busy to say the least. While chasing two rowdy boys and nursing a baby, a new and improved business plan came to light. As with most of my decisions, I usually take the plunge during the most inconvenient of times.

With three children and another on the way, I realized that the only way to ensure success was to combine expenses by reverting to the lost business model of a shopkeeper. We sold our new home and purchased a giant Queen Anne Victorian on the beautiful main street in our picturesque village. During this process we anticipated the arrival of the last Roefs child. It was while pregnant with my daughter Gracie that I opened my first consignment store out of our home.

CHAPTER 17
BITING YOUR TONGUE IN THE
NAME OF CUSTOMER SERVICE

There are days that I sincerely wonder about the human race. Some of my worst business moments stem from the most wretched shoppers. That includes both online shoppers and in-store consumers. In preparation for some of the most awkward situations you could imagine, I've compiled a few from over the years. As you read just be sure to think to yourself, "How would I handle myself in this situation?"

One unsolicited opinion came from a clearly unstable woman who had some unresolved issues in life. She approached me during one of my yearly charity drives for local homeless women. An often-overlooked need in the homeless community is feminine hygiene products. We would dedicate one month a year to collecting tampons and pads for the local food pantries as well as stocking the homeless shelter in our area. Our tampon drive has grown to be a wild success and I'm blessed with several supportive customers and consignors who help make it a reality. Out of nowhere this woman approached me, saying "I know why you are really doing this disgusting homeless drive!" Her smugness and odd smile suggested that this was not going to be a good thing. The only thing I could do was ask for clarification as to her meaning.

"You are secretly obsessed with vaginas! That's why!" She started to spit and sputter as she continued ranting to me about my less than honorable intentions. I hope no one else has ever encountered someone with this bizarre amount of rage over an innocent attempt to help those in need.

One of my greatest regrets in business is how I handled myself at this moment. How we handle ourselves with the public is always under scrutiny. That thought did not cross my mind as I was flushed with anger. Instead of anger, I wish I had looked her dead in the eye and said, "I'm sorry you feel that way but I'm just trying to make a difference in this ugly world." Short and sweet and to the point would have been a better option, but I was incapable as I felt personally attacked. What was wrong with that woman is the makings of an entirely different book. The point I'm trying to get across is that we will always have haters. People will always judge us. Learning to let it roll off our backs is not easy. This happened several years ago, and it still bothers me. Just when I think I've made great personal progress at not caring what others think of me, something will happen that reminds me that I still have a ways to go.

Take for instance the incident that happened earlier this week. Minding my own business on a snowy day, feeling festive that the holidays are upon us and all my children will be home for them, I'm trying to keep the door to my store closed as the heat is blowing full force to keep it warm inside. A woman is bringing items in to consign and has a few bags. When asked if she wants assistance, she denies help and insists she can do it alone. What she does to achieve this is to leave my door wide open while she meanders from her car to my store counter. This is letting gusting cold winds flow through the open door. My warm store is beginning to feel frosty. At this point I walk over and shut the door. She demands to know why I'm doing this. Having to explain that it's 30 degrees outside and my heat is on seems redundant, but I proceed to tell her. She looks me up and down and says, "Well you've got plenty of fat on you, so that shouldn't be a problem!"

Speechless is not an adjective my friends would ever use to describe me, however I was at that moment in time, truly speechless. My gaping mouth did nothing to indicate to her that I was utterly mortified at her statement. She continued on her merry way to my intake counter with her goods. As I walked, red faced, to my counter a thousand thoughts rushed through my head. Not many of them were that of a professional businesswoman but more of an upset little girl who had faced years of ridicule and assumptions.

Looking through her belongings it was difficult not to hurl insults at her. Making my way through her items for consignment was difficult. Thankfully her items were outdated and extremely worn which meant they were not acceptable for consignment.

Despite my tales, I am a firm believer in the idea that the customer is always right. Without the customer, we have no business. In consignment, the owner must answer to both the customer and the consignor. That's a lot of people to answer to. This is not always an easy feat. Have you ever noticed that most often a good deed goes unnoticed? Now go ahead and get into an argument with a customer and you could end up with viral infamy.

Years ago I had a young woman who spoke broken English come in to shop. Her small tots were with her and she seemed like a nice young woman. Shortly after she began shopping, my daughter, who was six at the time, came up to the counter and demanded a peanut butter and jelly sandwich. Not sure what prompted that, I explained she would have to wait until lunchtime. She then started crying that the other kids had one, why couldn't she. Then I noticed that the woman had broken out juice boxes and peanut butter and jelly sandwiches for her kids. They were essentially picnicking on my toy floor while their mom was in another room shopping.

This was a defining moment for me and for my business. While I watched the children begin to play with the toys and proceed to smear sticky jelly onto them, I started to crumble. As a mom of four very self-assured and boisterous children, I itched to scold them and make them clean it. My mom life was clearly a very different approach than this young woman's. Instead of crying or freaking out, I casually walked over to the kids and smiled. Then I took a package of baby wipes and cleaned their hands. After my intervention, there were only a few toys that were sticky and smeared. While I was entertaining those little ones alongside my daughter, the woman wandered back in. She tried apologizing in broken English to me. With extreme hesitancy I responded in Spanish. It had been years since I'd had a chance to use my high school Spanish.

The rusty vocabulary was a most welcome sound to this poor woman, who would eventually become a friend of mine. She was new to the United States and had no one to converse with except her husband until I came along. This was her first outing in a strange new place and she apologized for the mess. Being housebound with small children is something I am all too familiar with. My reaction to this situation could have gone in an entirely different direction. Choking down my initial frustration, I chose to extend a helping hand. That small act made a world of difference. From then on, I've always looked forward to our conversations. Never would I have forged that bond had I acted on my first impulse. Now those children are teens and they remain loyal customers.

CHAPTER 18
SENTIMENTAL JOURNEY

Something that will continually arise in this industry is battling sentimental attachments to inanimate objects. Always keep in mind that when a person brings you an item to sell, they have somehow come into possession of it. Either it was a gift, they purchased it, or sometimes they've inherited it and, in that case, they are even more emotional about it. What's important to keep in mind is that they somehow acquired that item. Tact is essential to not offend your consignor.

Once, before I owned a shop of my own, I overheard an employee at another consignment shop explain to an older woman why she was unable to accept her items for consignment. "These clothes are simply way too outdated!" Even to my novice ears at the time, I knew that was a horrible thing to say to a woman. Imagine how that woman felt, hearing that the clothing that she had taken the time to gather and cart in to your shop was worthless. In my experience, it has always been a much better business practice to blame it on the shoppers.

Some of my go to responses are to tell the truth in a kind way:

"I'm so sorry, but for some reason my shoppers don't seem to be buying this style."

"For some reason this particular style doesn't seem to sell well for us."

"These just don't seem to move, and I don't want to waste your time if it's not going to sell."

A warm encouraging word will forever be remembered, just as a blunt or harsh comment will stick with a person.

One of the things that sets me apart from other store owners is my very unassuming attire. This is my way of eloquently stating that my fashion leaves a lot to be desired. My little sister clearly got all the fashion genes. She is a leggy, beautiful blonde who doesn't appear to age, and her style makes her look like she just walked off the cover of Vogue magazine. Quite often she will watch my LIVE Facebook videos in horror and then text me and try to suggest how not to dress the next time. She tries but it just never sticks. My favorite fashion involves jeans and a comfy hoodie; throw on one of my worn and treasured baseball caps and I'm feeling like the star of my own movie.

It is a rough business, consignment, especially when you stock not only fashion but housewares and furniture as well. One moment I'm sorting Hermes scarves and Vince Camuto shoes, and the next I'm helping unload a truck of primitives that someone has cleaned out. A hoodie provides the luxury of adapting to both situations. Please note that the Hermes treasure is not an everyday occurrence but when it does happen, it makes my week.

CHAPTER 19
FINDING YOUR VOICE IN A NOISY WORLD

Sometimes the hardest thing to do is say NO. My father used to tell me that the hardest word in the dictionary was one of the shortest. He was right, and I don't often say that about him. If you stick to your ideals and your true business vision, you should see success. You will always have haters. It is inevitable, especially when you are in the spotlight. Being in business puts you in the public eye.

Sticking to your values and your business practices sounds simple, but can be surprisingly tough. There will be consignors and customers that challenge you to the core. Let them! No matter what situation I've gotten myself into over the years, there are people who embrace me and people who hate me. It took many years to not let the haters shake me to the point of non-functioning. My child, the House of Consignment, has given me my voice. It's given me the courage to stick to my values and speak up for myself and my business. If you can find a way to turn every hater into a motivator, you will surpass your competition.

As you enter the entrepreneurial world, many people of all different backgrounds will offer their advice. No matter what type of experience they come from, it's best to listen. That's not to say that you should act on every piece of advice. Sometimes someone will make a suggestion that will speak directly to you and help you out. In other cases, they will make some astounding suggestion that makes you wonder how they've managed to survive this far in life.

Listening to all of it has its advantages. An insane idea from someone with good intentions sometimes births the best ideas you'll ever have. There have been times when I was offered a suggestion and it hit me hard that it was a terrible idea. Yet the idea wouldn't go away, and I would subconsciously try to make that idea work and it would lead to a creative and insightful sales idea or marketing campaign. While you are figuring your way in this wild world of being an entrepreneur, don't be afraid of trying new things. As long as your heart is in the right place and you have good intentions, most will succeed, or at least help you figure out your market and develop your strategies.

When I first revealed my 12 months of charitable causes, people would smile and say, "how nice." Now, after years of exposing them to my zany drives and seeing the impact that the efforts made, people will call us and ask what the charity of the month is and how they can help. They email to be sure they are contributing. It's amazing how an idea I had to make a difference for one year of my business life has grown to be an intrinsic part of my business plan.

Not everyone was sold on my intentions at the beginning and that's ok. It was my job to show them how we could make a difference and to use my business as the catalyst.

CHAPTER 20
SIZE MATTERS

It never ceases to amaze me that a person driving a tiny car will attempt all sorts of insane tactics to move a larger piece of furniture to their home. Once I witnessed a woman loading a six-foot tall wooden pressboard bookcase into her Volkswagen trunk. Since half was inside her trunk she felt it wasn't necessary to strap it in. Despite all attempts to persuade her to simply tie the case in, she wouldn't hear of it. Two miles later, I got the phone call from her furious that it had fallen out and was laying in pieces all over the road. She was demanding a full refund. The ludicrousness of that statement didn't even faze me. Before you wonder too long, no, I did not issue her a refund. There are times when you must draw the line.

Through the years, I've longed to sell furniture

of all styles. One of my favorite things to do is display all the smalls on the vast array of furniture that gets consigned. Unfortunately I came to the sad conclusion that large furniture just didn't sell well at my shop. For whatever reason, it took forever to move a large piece whereas smaller pieces were moving extremely well. My stubbornness kept me lugging bulky pieces for a few more years until I finally wised up and changed my tune.

My moment of awakening happened on a sunny Saturday. Shoppers were out in full force taking advantage of the nice weather. A woman had discovered a large primitive armoire and was gushing with delight. She promptly paid for the armoire and promised to be right back with her husband and his truck. Shortly after they returned together. Her husband was a muscular man who could have loaded the armoire all on his own as his arms were the size of small tree trunks. As he lit his cigarette and leaned against my store's porch railing, he made the snarky comment, "Since you sold it to her, you two can load it yourselves!"

The woman was obviously embarrassed, and I turned bright red. He probably assumed I was red from embarrassment. No, I was red faced from a furious temper boiling just under the surface. His nasty tone and condescending demeanor did not sit well with me. For some insane reason, I went along with this plan and we struggled to load the armoire with him watching. As he chuckled when it got hung up when we attempted to place it in the bed of his truck, something in me began to unravel. While struggling with the piece, which was now completely hung up on his tailgate, I heard him laugh and say, "Now where you gonna go with that?" With the biggest shove I could muster, the armoire went skidding across his tailgate. While this episode infuriated me, it did help decide the fate of large furniture in my shop. We were officially done selling large bulky pieces. From that day forward, we only consigned pieces that two women could easily place in the back of an SUV or van. As far as that shopper goes, she still visits my shop to this day. They're still married, and she has never brought him back, for which I thank my lucky stars.

For all the horror stories, keep in mind that there are hundreds of amazing stories. Stories of happy customers and consignors that made my business what it is today. The important thing to learn from this story is that it helped me to define my business. The most awful situations are the ones you can learn the most from. By clearly redefining my policies and terms of acceptance, I was able to prevent anything like that happening again. Keep this in mind the next time chaos hits. Think to yourself, after the dust settles, how could I have avoided this? What should I do to prevent it in the future?

CHAPTER 21
COMPETITION IS GOOD

In my entrepreneurship infancy, I was frightened by competition. Whether this can be attributed to my upbringing or to my lack of business sense, I'm not sure. Let me clarify that I'm in no way suggesting you run out and share all your knowledge and help your competition do a better job than you. However, by keeping open lines of communications with them, you will build a strong business network.

When I was in the beginnings of my brick and mortar store, I was very unsure of myself. Let's chalk it up to being young and inexperienced. One of my good friends opened another consignment shop near me. It rocked me to the core and made me feel extremely fearful. What I should have done was embrace it and grown both of us. It took me years to relax. In my defense, she was a marketing professional with years more experience than me. My family was also dependent on my income at that point. My fears outweighed all else; fight or flight instinct took over.

Thankfully, the years passed and both our businesses thrived. We have buried the hatchet (not in each other) and have grown to work together making a bigger impact. Our businesses actually complement one another and only help us reach a larger audience. We (and our town) are a destination, and by working together we can demonstrate that to both current and potential customers. For all my poor decisions along the road, I'm glad this situation was remedied. We are both better off for it.

Working alongside the others in your industry is imperative for growth. There are two resale organizations that I belong to. Both are unique in their own ways. The knowledge you can glean from others who understand exactly what you are going through is invaluable. If you ever get to the point that you feel you have learned all you can, you're probably not going to be in business much longer. The process of growth should never stop, in any business, if you are planning for longevity. This world doesn't stop turning. We must adapt and continue to grow our business practices, or we will cease to exist in this noisy world.

CHAPTER 22
CONSTRUCTIVE CRITICISM:
TAKE IT LIKE A CHAMP

One of the harshest reality checks I've had was when a good friend in the industry came out for a visit to my store. Angie Houloose owns Absolutely Her in Omaha, Nebraska. If you have ever visited her store you will understand that she has an amazing gift. Her displays are outstanding and her storefront windows rival that of the stores on Fifth Avenue. As I was feeling a bit stale, I needed her honesty. Whether you have a brick and mortar or an online store, having the critique of a fresh set of eyes is an excellent way to polish your image. That said, it's easier said than done.

Personally, I shed many a tear when she gave me her opinion. So try to learn from your mistakes and not let your ego stand in the way of progress. It was never that she was mean to me. She was honest, and her honesty was accurate. Have you ever had a deep-down gut feeling that there was a problem with a certain situation, but you chose to ignore it simply because it was easier? Angie's visit brought my deepest concerns to light and it was uncomfortable, to say the least. Growth is not always comfortable, however it is essential to address areas to improve.

One of her initial assessments of my shop was that I had dust bunnies. Having four floors of consignment is not easy to maintain. It's all I can do to manage the day-to-day duties, and then throw in employees and I'm shot. Hearing the truth aloud from my peer was tough. Did I mention that just that one observation made me cringe and cry? Do I still have dust bunnies? No, I do not. (Well, there are still a few roaming, but the size of the herd has decreased significantly). It's now on a task list to keep on top of those breeding fools and try to keep them to a minimum. Whether your cringe worthy point is a dust bunny or poorly lit photos, you must be aware of areas in which you could improve. This is just another part of the key evolution of your business. Don't we all want to create the best business possible? Accepting constructive criticism is a great opportunity to achieve that.

My children have always been my motivation and my biggest fans. They've also been my harshest critics and sharpest thorns in my side. Growing the business around them, there's no escaping the fact that they understand certain business principles. They've lived through a variety of insane employee issues, customer drama, business dilemmas and all that goes with it. As they got older, they began to form hard views on how certain things should be handled.

One wintry day, my youngest child Gracie was playing in the store while I worked. This was a normal occurrence. She always had to have some sort of involvement with the store. She was literally born into the store business. As she played with her toys, she was observing an employee at work. This employee was plodding along and not setting the world on fire. It drove me to distraction, as I had a hundred things on my mind.

Let's back up and make clear that being a boss was never my strong suit. Confrontation is tough and not in my list of job skills. After the workday ended and the employee had left for home, in a matter of fact voice, my daughter said, "She has to go! Mom! You need to fire her! She makes you work harder!" She was 10 and knew the woman needed to be let go. Deep down I knew this but the fear of being down a staffer and having to fire this woman kept me from making a necessary business decision. The next day I fired the woman and felt immediate relief that I was no longer flushing her wages down the toilet. My 10 year old recognized that and forced me to face my deep seated fear; firing is not an easy thing to do. To this day I'm not a fan of it. No matter how difficult it feels to do, sometimes it is necessary for the larger picture.

Are you open to suggestions? Do you listen to your peers, your customers, your family? I'm extremely grateful to have a supportive family. My husband has always been my biggest champion. He's also the voice of reason. Recently I went live on Facebook and joked (outwardly was joking but deep down I would love a larger storefront) about needing him to find me a larger location. Deadpan, he quickly retorted that I needed to have a sale instead. All joking aside, he keeps me grounded and helps me work through my ideas instead of jumping head first into a decision that could potentially ruin my business.

The flip side of this is to not let the Negative Nellies in your life bring you down. There are some people who cannot fathom change or a leap of faith. Those people don't have any business being in business. It takes a special breed of person to tackle owning their own business. There definitely is not a lot of security with a startup business. Keep in mind that not everyone will be your cheerleader on the road to success.

CHAPTER 23

IF I'M GOING TO SPEND $1,500 ON LOUIS, I'D BETTER BE SLEEPING WITH HIM

Blame it all on my roots, (sing it, Garth) but I just don't think I could handle coughing up $1,500 for a used luxury handbag. Who am I kidding? Louis would have a fabulous home with me but I just can't afford him. Don't let this discourage you. We are all different in our unique way. Every single resale shop offers their clientele a slightly different experience. After all, that is the small business key to success, to create an experience that can't be duplicated by the big box stores. Some of my most treasured resale friends carry a high-end inventory that I can't even fathom.

Once, in Las Vegas, I fondled my friend Vena's brand new Louis Vuitton while she was in the restroom and had left him unattended at the table. From what I can estimate, that bag cost more than my first automobile. It's all relative. High-end stores have a different image to set forth than that of a middle class American shop like mine. It was exhilarating to sling him over my shoulder and smell his leathery luxury. If I were to carry a bag like that, my customers would feel like I was a bit pretentious. This is not meant in a mean way at all. It just further reinforces that you must understand your target market.

During my infancy stages of business, I traveled to my sister's home in the state of Maryland with the entire family. She recommended I check out a luxury shop in downtown Frederick. With glee, I fled with George and left her to care for four rowdy youngsters. As we entered the high-end boutique, we immediately realized we were not in our element. Glamorous doesn't even begin to explain the feeling. Designer labels were showcased everywhere. To be honest, several of the names were unknown to me. This was not my comfort zone and I began to wish I had never come. As I searched out George to try and flee, a beautiful blonde woman approached me. She was dressed to perfection. She was flawless. She looked as if she had just stepped off a runway. That was how I became acquainted with Ellen Didion, owner of Chic to Chic. What followed was an inspiring moment that helped me grow on so many levels.

To set the tone, please remember my fashion stylings and envision me standing there in a hoodie. This was one of those moments that I wished I had been given my sister's fashion sense. To my surprise, not only did this woman seem unfazed by my attire, she greeted me with sincere warmth. It soon became clear that she had a passion for making her customers feel fabulous about themselves. That day I purchased an incredible dress and several accessories. As I left her boutique, I felt like a million dollars. Aside from purchasing a dress that I would have not normally bought, I was struck with how much lighter I felt as I left. The shopping experience at Chic to Chic had altered my business vision forever. It made me start to take a closer look at the shopping experience in my own store. While I do not carry such high-end items, I do carry what my customers want. This experience led me to try and create that atmosphere in my own market.

Years later, at a resale conference, I would meet up with Ellen again. Ellen is still the same enthusiastic and forward thinking entrepreneur today. Her fortitude in this industry gives me strength despite the fact that we are from two very different markets. Our friendship has taught me that there is much to be learned from a variety of experiences. Adapting and learning from successful business models, such as Ellen's, can help you find your own path. While I may never sell a Louis Vuitton, you can rest assured that when a customer leaves my store with their purchases, we will have done all we could have to ensure they left with that same feeling as having just bought a Louis.

CHAPTER 24
TO CONSIGN OR NOT TO CONSIGN

This chapter is dedicated to one of my very best consignors, #1187. She has impeccable taste and loves to scour all the local thrifts and yard sales for her eBay store. Her eBay store was an inspiration to me and let me live vicariously. Despite the success of my brick and mortar shop, I always missed the eBay auction excitement. Many people in this life will have a fake persona in which their world is rosy and perfect. #1187 was always down to earth and we hit it off. Her forward-thinking attitude and positive ways were always a treat. She didn't sugar coat life and I felt myself sharing with her. Soon I would divulge all the different hot selling tickets and trends as they were happening. She would share her online experiences with me and was an immense help with my fast track to learning more about jewelry and what to look for.

She is one person I would be genuinely happy to see, to look through her stuff. Whatever didn't sell online, for whatever reason, she would bring to me. Most often, it was high end and didn't fetch a high enough price. Being able to offer these brands to my shoppers was a godsend. When I explained the term "picker" to her, she chuckled.

Another fabulous consignor is #2320. She likes to shop all sorts of resale shops and brings in a large amount of name brand items. Her quest to keep on top of the consignment trends is incredible. She will usually haul in a few totes at a time. When she does, my employees panic for various reasons. Firstly, she has so much and we all fully realize that 99% of it will be accepted. She takes great pride in sorting and cleaning the items before they enter our store. Secondly, she will ask for explanations on why we did not accept the other 1% of items for consignment. While my staff feels intimidated, I feel elated that she is paying attention. Essentially she is making my job easier as she won't make the same mistake twice. It also keeps us on our toes as to what is moving and what is not.

Some of my consignors have been conducting business with me for nearly 20 years. How did my relationships with these consignors go so many years without me acknowledging them? Our consignors and pickers especially are the core of our existence. Without them and their wares, I would have no inventory, and thus no business. It became my goal that year to find a way to thank them. First, I had to determine whom exactly to thank.

Obviously, there were a few who I knew were at the top of the list. I found that I could run a report in my software that would tell me the top 10 consignors of my business. A few on that list were complete surprises to me – make sure you understand and use all the capabilities of your software!

Next question—how to thank them? Various ideas went through my head. It was nearing Christmas and I wanted to surprise the top ten consignors with something memorable. A local restaurant gift certificate, movie passes, etc. seemed too easy. When a consignor brings in items, they're usually in grocery bags, boxes, and whatever else they have lying around. They write their consignor number on the bags or boxes, and it's not exactly an elegant process. One day it hit me—I would buy ten quality tote bags from a local at-home consultant and have their consignor numbers embroidered on the front of the bags. Perfect!

Waiting for those bags to come in seemed to take forever. The excitement was unbearable. The looks on their faces when they opened their gifts (yes, I wrapped them), was priceless. #1187 gave me the most sincere smile and said, "This is the best gift I've received in years." What a smashing success! Those consignors are still my best sources. Remember, it only takes a little effort to solidify your relationships with your top consignors. What could you do to thank a consignor today?

CHAPTER 25
GIVING BACK MAKES A DIFFERENCE

I've said that my upbringing left me with little tolerance for seeing people go without. Please don't take that to mean that I feel sad about my childhood. It's simply that there is such a vast gap between those who have and those who have not. There are so many ways in which everyone can help those less fortunate.

It hit me one year that instead of donating unsold items to various charities and burdening them with the task of turning unsaleable goods into profit, I should rethink the entire process. My business at that time had grown to a point where I had a staff and a bit of energy to devote to something other than strict consignment. Little did I know that my charitable desire would grow to be the biggest component to my business model.

CHAPTER 26
IT ALL STARTED WITH A TAMPON

It all started with a tampon. While googling homelessness and researching needs in local communities, it came to my attention that tampons and pads were scarce in shelters. Women were more susceptible to infection and disease when they were unable to properly take care of their periods. Considering my own period and realizing how very fortunate I was to be able to afford the items I found necessary was a sobering moment. I shuddered at the appalling thought of another woman unable to procure the simplest of hygiene necessities. Having the best intentions, I began to feel out the public. To my astonishment, many people (of both genders) are embarrassed at the thought of discussing tampons in public. I'm not much of a prude, so this didn't deter me.

My first attempt was to host an after-hours sales event for which the cost of admittance was a box of tampons. It was clearly a tampon drive but I longed for catchy name. Surprisingly, the most amazing idea came from our local chemistry teacher, John. He jokingly suggested, "No Strings Attached" should be the theme of the party. It spoke to my soul and from that point forward, our annual efforts were called the No Strings Attached party.

Our first year we collected a little over 4,000 tampons, which we delivered to the local homeless shelter. The second year, we did the same event and it grew to 6,000 tampons. The third year we did the No Strings Attached party and combined it with a "tampon terror trip". This trip was a chartered bus to a haunted attraction right before Halloween. We sold the tickets and included commemorative t-shirts and merchandise. On the 220-mile trek to the haunted prison we sold raffle tickets for various fun and exciting prizes we had on board. All together we raised over 8,000 tampons.

The next year I was determined to hit 10,000 tampons. Mixing it up, I approached the local drive-in movie theatre and asked to rent their venue. We held the event in September and played classic family Halloween movies, *Hocus Pocus* and *Ghostbusters*. Our event spiraled out of control on Facebook with its reach extending farther than I could have ever imagined. The night of the event the weather was perfect and the drive-in was sold out. People were parking on the road outside the fences and walking in with their donations. It was one of the best nights of my life. To see an idea come to life and exceed your wildest dreams is humbling. We started the night out with my husband's 8-foot truck bed empty and by the end of the night it was overflowing. The cost of admission was simple: a box of tampons or pads per person. After a few years of talking about the uncomfortable topic of menstruation, people were used to my efforts. The majority of attendees brought not one but multiple boxes of products to donate.

Our event was a smashing success, with a final count of tampons and pads at 24,541. We were able to not only stock the three local homeless shelters, but four different food pantries as well. The events success helped the House of Consignment brand reach a much larger audience. All staff was on hand, in costume, to run the event and answer questions about the world of consignment.

CHAPTER 27
DIAPER DEPRIVATION

With the success of the first year's tampon drive, I was fueled to find other ways I could make a difference. It became clear to me that people really do want to help, but they need to be shown how. With some effort on my part, if I made it easy for them to help, it would make a greater impact. This was how the diaper drive was hatched.

While researching the concerns of homelessness, I discovered there is a term called diaper deprivation. This is not exclusive to homeless women. In fact, one in three mothers suffer from anxiety about how they will afford to diaper their child. Imagine having to choose between diapering your child or feeding them. The thought alone makes me depressed.

We decided to collect diapers of all sizes

throughout the month. Often moms would bring in diapers that had never been opened as their children had outgrown them before they could be used. As an added incentive, we ran a special around Easter. I bought an Easter bunny costume and we offered FREE photos with the Easter bunny for a special one-day event. We suggested donations of diapers in all marketing for the event. This accommodated the families who could simply not afford to purchase photos. They would receive a printed photo by a professional photographer for free, with the option of purchasing a photo package for an additional fee. The additional package was almost always purchased. This helped to compensate the photographer. This boosted our collection of diapers, and also proved to be an excellent way to give my shop added exposure. We have continued with an annual Easter diaper drive as a result. If you try a diaper drive, be sure the call the shelter ahead of time, and ask which size diapers are in the greatest demand.

My own experience with cloth diapers was horrific, and my husband made me swear to never attempt it again. With every good intention, I set forth to diaper my youngest son Bryden in cloth diapers. Not sure what to do with a soiled cloth diaper, I decided to try and roll the majority of the mess into the toilet. My older son, Tristin, was horrified, and proceeded to question me to death. "Why are you playing in the toilet?" made it hard to focus on the task. Eventually, Tristin flushed the toilet and somehow it sucked down the cloth diaper. My reflexes kicked in and I plunged my hands into the bowl to try and save the diaper. Disgusting, I know, and my son will no doubt be in therapy over it. We shared a moment over that toilet bowl, both of us in shock over what we had just witnessed. Suddenly it seemed as though the cloth diaper movement had gotten the best of me. My husband had to tear the toilet apart to fish the diaper out that night. There was lots of swearing and grumbling as that diaper gave him a run for his money. At the end of night, my son Tristin summed it up perfectly as he whined, "I don't like those diapers!" Many capable mothers are able to use them and there are even diaper services available (for a substantial fee) in metropolitan areas. For many of us, it is so much simpler and cleaner to use disposable diapers. More importantly, it's an economic issue. A mother who is working full time and caring for her children cannot spend the time or even access the equipment to properly clean cloth diapers. The initial investment in them is also considerable.

Upon the completion of the last diaper drive, I enlisted the help of my husband. Together we made the diaper deliveries. What a rewarding sense of accomplishment this was. We were helped with the unloading by a young mother who was in tears of relief over the delivery. As we drove home that night, I could tell that my husband had begun to understand the bigger picture; our efforts were actually making a difference. This is something we don't take lightly.

CHAPTER 28
THANK A VETERAN TODAY

While working through the initial phases of my charitable drives, other areas of need came to light. The local veterans' home was full of elderly men and women who had served our country. Aside from raising money, I wanted to make an impact, and make my donors understand that they were part of the process of making a difference.

Originally, I intended to collect new hats and other accessories for donation. However, as with the homeless drive, I decided to do my own research and dig a little deeper. Turns out that the veterans' home had a very popular painting class. They loved to paint, and I was granted access to sit in on one such class. Veterans of all different levels of health were in attendance. Clearly the outlet of art was much appreciated and needed at this facility.

With some communication with the activities coordinator and the director of the home, we were able to figure out what items would most benefit this art class. They needed paints of a certain brand that met with compliance guidelines. They also needed canvas boards to paint on, as well as paint brushes. They were painting on anything and everything including cardboard and older works of art that had been spray-painted white. It didn't bother them. They simply wanted to paint. That first year I asked for donations of paints, brushes and canvas boards. I had a barely mediocre response. Many people wanted to help, but they would buy the wrong brand of paints and we weren't able to donate them due to restrictions. To make the greatest impact it was clear that I had to make it as easy as possible for donors to help.

In May of the next year we decorated a Christmas tree in red, white and blue lights. We made our own paper decorations. It wasn't anything extravagant at all. All I did was use the address label option on my word processor. I created a decent-sized label complete with an American flag on the left side of the tag with name and phone number to the right. I printed out a bunch on three different colored sheets of paper: red, white and blue. We punched a hole in a corner and tied a gold string to make it into an ornament. Anyone could purchase an "ornament" for our patriotic tree for $1 apiece. The money raised went to purchase acrylic paints for the veterans' home. We kept it simple and devoted the entire month of May to it.

By Memorial Day, our tree was heavily laden with ornaments of red, white and blue. It helped to have donors see the actual progress and I made sure to insist that they fill out their ornament's information and hang it on the tree themselves. Quite often they would purchase several ornaments and not just one. It was a happy day when I was able to deliver a few hundred bottles of paint to the veterans. Of course, to ensure the future success of this drive, I took photos of the end result of all our efforts. This photo was then shared with all who helped make this drive a success.

CHAPTER 29
HOMELESS EFFORTS

For a smaller effort that still creates a meaningful impact, consider a small display on your countertop that sells something the area homeless need, like lip balm. Simple signage explains that for each lip balm sold, you will donate one to the local homeless shelter. We took it a step further and took a plastic container and labeled it for the shelter. As customers made their purchases, we let them drop a lip balm into the container designated for the shelter. This drives home the impact they are making, which your consignment shop is facilitating. Make a person feel good about themselves and that sticks with them.

Let's chat about dirty socks. Did you have any idea that one of the most needed items at a homeless shelter is socks? Think about your own feet and socks. What do you do when your feet get wet? You change to dry socks! A homeless person who only owns one pair of tattered socks is unable to do this. Some of their most essential needs are not obvious to someone who isn't in that position. When I learned that, I made it my mission to bring those needs into the light and get those socks donated! My first attempt was a mess. I worded everything wrong and made the mistake of broadcasting far and wide that I was looking for sock donations. In addition, I offered every donor of a pair of socks a raffle ticket and a chance to win a beautiful raffle basket. What I didn't anticipate was that most people would donate old, used socks. While they were (for the most part) freshly laundered, it didn't sit well with me. The irony is that the first time I delivered these socks to a shelter they were gratefully received. Nevertheless, I decided to work towards a better drive in which I could give homeless people, already down on their luck, a pair of new socks. It seemed like the least I could do.

It took me a while, but I was able to figure out a plan to make that happen. This led me to research the wholesale market and find reputable sources for quality socks at an affordable price. If I was able to secure a certain price, then I could offer to sell the socks to the public, and for each pair of socks they purchased, they would be purchasing a pair for us to donate to our local shelter. When the day came to launch, the idea was well received and was only more fun because you were helping others by buying yourself a fun new pair of socks. This promotion offered the best of both worlds! Make it easy for your customers to make a difference while branding your business.

CHAPTER 30
PUPPIES AND KITTIES AND CATNIP, OH MY!

Unlike tampons and diapers, I can with absolute certainty tell you that assisting local animal shelter pets is uncontroversial. People are quick to jump on board those drives. We have tried a few different drives and we try to devote two months per year to helping local animals. We collect cleaning supplies, raise money for dog and cat food, you name it.

At the insistence of my oldest daughter Jorja (the biggest animal lover I've ever produced), we decided to make pet toys for the animals in the shelter one year for Christmas. That girl has a huge heart and I wasn't about to let her down. We started searching for animal safe toys that wouldn't take a lot of time to make. We narrowed it down to something we could easily make at little to no cost: braided cloth rope toys for dogs. To cut costs we used cotton T-shirts that were unsaleable. We discovered that there was a specific way in which to cut the T-shirt that would turn it into one long continual strand of fabric. We then braided them into beefy ropes. Jorja was super excited to deliver them to the dogs at the shelter right before Christmas. Once they were donated, she asked if we could make them to sell and give the money to the shelter. Her tenacity was irresistible, and I'm still not sure where she gets it from. We set up an old-fashioned sewing bee type event with local friends and family. In one day, we were able to cut, braid and complete around a hundred dog ropes to sell in our shop. The first year, we sold a ton of the dog ropes to all sorts of pet owners and we used that money to buy dog food at wholesale cost through our locally owned and run pet store.

The next year Jorja upped the ante and pushed me to do something for the cats at the shelter. We went back to the drawing board and found catnip squid shaped toys for cats. It involved lots of cutting, sewing and stuffing. Again we set up our sweat shop of friends and family, and created a little over a hundred of these catnip toys. First we donated several to the local shelter and then we went to selling them. Our goal was to sell enough that we could have a cat communal built. A cat communal is a structure that allows several cats to live in a group setting. This provides the cats with a sense of control over their environment as opposed to a cage. It allows them to engage in feline behaviors, which reduces their stress while adapting to shelter life. My daughter now volunteers at the very same shelter. It does my heart good to see my children going out and contributing to society in ways that are meaningful to them.

Our trial run nearly killed our geriatric cat, Chimney. Her normal day consisted of lounging, harassing our small herd of King Charles dogs and demanding more food. A cat's life is rough. After all, they can't seem to ever eat food out of a bowl that isn't rounded on top and heaven help you should the bottom of the bowl be visible through the food. Unacceptable! Well, it seems the one-pound bag of bulk catnip I ordered shook her back to the days of her youth. The morning after its arrival, we woke to discover what a catatonic state actually looks like. All the dogs were looming over our cat in shock as she lay on her back in a fully sedated state of mind. Sometime during the night she had managed to chew a hole in the bag of catnip and slip into a high that lasted almost two days. After that, we were sure to store all catnip in a sealed glass jar and keep it out of sight and smell.

CHAPTER 31
CANCER CARE PACKAGES

I love to sew, but by no means am I a seamstress or even a highly skilled sewing enthusiast. Some of my fondest memories are of listening to my grandmother's vintage Singer sewing machine humming along. She did her best to teach me the skill. Fortunately, I learned the basics and it's gotten me through a few projects.

It wasn't until I had children that I realized all that I could do with a sewing machine. With fabric I've been able to make costumes, super hero capes with trains on them, 18" doll clothing because I couldn't afford the real deal, and more. When my sophisticated youngest daughter Gracie cried because we couldn't find a pencil skirt in her tiny size, I went to work and it is one of my biggest claims to fame that she not only loved the skirt I made her but she wore it to a middle school dance. Those of you with teenage children can appreciate the enormity of that!

Sewing took on a new purpose as the catnip creations came to life. From there we looked for other projects to sew that would benefit people in need. I came to realize I had an alarmingly large customer base of people with cancer of all different sorts, and thus was born the charity event nearest and dearest to my heart. We decided to create cancer care packages for people embarking on their path of chemotherapy and radiation treatments. So often people enter their first day of treatment with a great fear of the unknown. Our care packages are there to reassure them that they are not alone. Our carefully thought out packages also provide treasures to keep them occupied during the inevitably long waits for treatment.

I researched the care packages by talking to some of my dear friends who were going through the toughest time of their lives. I didn't relish asking hard questions about how they felt, but in order to make this work, I needed to know what they actually wanted. The list started out quite lengthy as each cancer patient offered up various suggestions. Combining those lists and realizing which items they all had in common helped me to create what I feel is a most effective package. From there I put out that list and asked for donations. This was extremely well received by our entire community, not just my customer base. I was invited to speak at a few local community service groups. Not only did this further my cause, but it gained me several new customers and they were not only consigning but they were donating the most amazing amounts of goods for the packages. Our efforts were written about in local papers and the momentum grew. Soon we had several hundred items. One person anonymously donated 11 large boxes of supplies that were drop-shipped from Amazon. The need was there, and the response was clear—people wanted to make this a success. We pressed on, all the while running the shop in its normal capacity. On top of all the smalls we could fill the care packages with, we wanted to take it a step further.

From our many discussions with cancer patients we had found that an infusion port can be very uncomfortable. A cancer treatment port is used to reduce the number of needle sticks a person's veins must endure, and allows for less wear and tear on their body. The port is most often located on the upper chest just below the collarbone. The port can be an uncomfortable piece of equipment and especially irritating while wearing a seatbelt. For some women, wearing a bra is difficult as the strap rubs against it. A port pillow can help alleviate the pain and nuisance of having a port. It's a small pillow with a hook-and-loop fastener that you can use on your seatbelt to cushion the port or even wear on a bra strap. This simple but valuable little device is not yet readily available.

With some digging we found several online

patterns for different styles of port pillows. We made a few samples and gave them to a few friends who were wearing ports at the time. We asked for sincere feedback, and we got it; they preferred a particular size, and they also wanted to keep the samples as they were a huge comfort to them during this phase of treatment. We set out to create a bunch, but we were quickly discouraged. We weren't really set up for mass production. The first year I was lucky enough to have caught the attention of my friend Jess who was a Home and Careers teacher. Not only did she help me by sewing up a bunch of port pillows, but she taught me how to efficiently make them to save time. This spurred me on to make more the following year. However, full-time work at the store in addition to all the charity work was beginning to make me lose my bearings. Stubbornly, I refused to back down on anything. It was then that I was approached by a local woman, Missy who asked if she could assist me in any way with my sewing. Her help and the donation of her time and effort made it possible for me to continue with my mission.

CHAPTER 32
CHARITABLE MINDSET

It's important to know that not only do charity drives help out locals in need but they help to solidify a relationship between you and your customer community. Working alongside one another for the greater good is something that makes your business appeal on a personal level. It also puts good karma out there for you and your store. That's something I try not to mess with.

Am I suggesting you attempt all of these charitable drives? Of course not, but I do want to make it clear how incorporating one or two charitable events a year can improve your business, your visibility in the community, and your connection with customers and consignors. I've met some of my very best consignors through my charitable work.

CHAPTER 33
LET'S GET SOCIAL!

The business model that I set out to create back in 1996 is certainly not the same today. There are so many factors that play into the growth and change of your business. Technology plays a very important part in the success of an ever-evolving business climate. It is up to the business owner to determine which social media sites their particular customer is using. You must be able to read the needs of your business and adapt as necessary.

Another vital aspect of this is to follow other businesses' social media. Keep your finger on the pulse of your industry. This does not mean to copy exactly as they do. Just being open to new ideas or products will help you stand apart. I have to admit that one of my most effective learning tools is to learn from others mistakes. If I'm watching a video or see a post that literally makes me cringe, I take note of it. Immediately reflect and ask yourself, "What about that post made me pause?" Often this will lead you to an improved idea of a post or video.

CHAPTER 34
SOCIAL MEDIA STRATEGY

Social media strategy is a plan for all you wish to create and achieve on social media. You need to clearly define your plan while keeping it a true reflection of your company's goals. For example, House of Consignment is a feel good space where people come to not only save money but to enjoy themselves. This has transcended into my online presence. Our store page is not simply a sales tool. We share all sorts of content that contains humor, money saving tips, and did I mention humor? This is not to say that we don't showcase our inventory or promote sales. We make a priority of posting content that will amuse our followers. There are so many pages to follow in today's busy world of social media. We make it our goal to stand out from the typical advertising pages.

The first step is to clearly define your goals. Yes, you read that correctly. You should have a few different goals. There are all sorts of goals to consider while you formulate your strategy. Address your business goals or your social media purpose won't be clear.

The world of social media is very large and complex. It is crucial that you determine which sites to spend your energy on. Doing a few extremely well will have considerably more impact than doing multitudes in a mediocre way. Keep in mind that social media is very fickle and constantly changing, so be ready to assess how productive your efforts are and refocus if necessary.

Whom exactly will you be targeting? Know your customer so that you are able to speak to them and engage them in your business. Social media is an excellent way to get to know them better. All business owners need to know what topics their customers love to see in their news feed.

Organic strategy is the art of creating such awesome content that your followers do the work of engaging for you. If you post something that truly speaks to them then they will like your post and hopefully comment. This lets the social media site's algorithms know people want to see your post, and the site will show your post to more people. Success breeds success. If your followers share the post on their timeline then that post just grew to superstar status. All the friends of that follower will now see your post and your branding. You just got FREE visibility in the world of social media.

To create an impactful social media strategy, first decide on a specific goal for each site. Each social media site is unique, with its own algorithms, procedures, layout, user base and personality. Decide on specific goals for each platform you use. Be specific and detailed. Setting a goal of "more sales" is too vague and doesn't force you to home in on specific strategies that will work for you. Dig deeper into what you actually hope to achieve. A better, more focused goal might be "drive more traffic to my brick and mortar store, thereby increasing sales." An even better goal would be "drive more traffic to my brick and mortar store in order to increase sales in my clothing department." This last goal forces you to key in to your followers' clothing needs. Show them how your store meets their needs, and why they have to shop with you.

You've set the goal, and now you have to go about making that goal a reality. Creating a game plan is much easier if you have your end goal in sight. Let's stick with the specific goal of "driving more traffic to my brick and mortar store in order to increase sales in my clothing department." You need to show them the savings and the value in shopping with your particular store. The best way to approach this is through subtle selling. If I'm creating a game plan for my clothing department, I try to showcase my product without it feeling like hard-sell ad. One way to do this is to ask their opinion!

Polls are excellent for showcasing items. Keep it simple and ask the question, "Which style do you prefer?" Offer two options. For example, one could be a comfortable dressy shoe while the other is a high heeled fashionable shoe. There is no right or wrong answer, but people love to give opinions! Do this in the POLL mode, which allows them to vote and immediately see how their choice is doing.

Here's what I would do. Create a quality photo that is branded (use your watermark which is easily achievable with one of the many apps available) to further reinforce your store.

The best photo is a real one from your own stock. Have a camera hungry staffer who loves to pose? Let them be the star and get them to model an outfit. Even if you have a camera shy staffer, offer to crop the photo to only show the outfit. Having an outfit on a real person or mannequin allows prospective shoppers to see how it actually looks on.

People are more likely to engage with a photo when it's homemade, so to speak. If I want to promote winter coats, this is an excellent opportunity to dress the model with not only a coat, but accessories as well. A glint of a necklace showing from between the coats lapels, a scarf draped down the sides, a pair of winter gloves holding a name brand purse. Make use of every single post for largest impact. The more you do this, the more comfortable you become. Above all else, you must remember that a photo is essential at minimum. People don't pause scrolling through their feed unless there's a photo or video. By having a fabulous photo, you are ensuring that they at least slow down while plowing through the many posts.

If you listen to all the various online sources, they will give you an array of days and times which will yield the best visibility for your posts. It's my humble opinion that each business has a very unique market. Sounds repetitive, doesn't it? Every single business owner must embrace what sets them apart from the pack. That's because if you want to survive this wild ride of being an entrepreneur, you have to get to know the patterns of your customers. Does a large majority of your customers work manufacturing on second or third shift? Are the majority stay-at-home moms? Do your customers work a high powered nine-to-five job which allows them lunch time access and late evening? When are your posts yielding the best results? These are all variants that you shouldn't be afraid of testing.

Now let's chat video and social media. Some people are terrified of going live or even creating a video. One of my good friends, Janna Sewell of Stillgoode Consignments in Texas, cracks me up as she films the items showcased in her store. At all costs she avoids any mirrors or surfaces that will show her reflection or image. Last I checked she wasn't a vampire so I'm assuming she suffers from a twinge of stage fright. This actually works in her favor as sometimes I want to watch her videos for the simple thrill of trying to catch her reflection as she is filming! If I do this then I am sure others are too. More importantly, Janna is putting herself and her family business out there. Each of us brings our unique twist to social media. Having the fortitude to go forward and do it is all that matters.

If you do experience stage fright or you just want a new angle to create eye catching video, there are several apps which allow you to do that using photos. How wonderful all this modern technology is, especially when it's easy to utilize. One of these apps is Legend and it's my go to method for a quick message. Using one photo, it allows you to insert a message and then lets you review the various ways in which to transform it into an eye catching motion video clip. This process is super easy and helps cut through the clutter of the many posts people see. It gets them to pause to see what message you are trying to convey.

Once you have a photo or video to go with, you are ready for the next step, wording to drive home your intention. How will you leave an impact on your viewer? There are an assortment of methods in which you could use. Mixing it up and utilizing a variety of these methods is the best way to not appear stale. If you use the same posting method, it will only keep them scrolling right past you in their news feed.

A call to action is an important way to motivate shoppers as well as track the success of your strategies. In order to track which methods are drawing the best responses, we must enact a call to action. This call to action is when you create content for a follower or reader and invite them to perform a specific act such as click here, shop now, visit us, etc. By suggesting they click here or shop now, you are furthering your engagement with them.

Just as important as a game plan is documenting your successes. Recording and being aware of what works for your unique followers is essential in order to connect with them. If you are unsure what motivates them then now is the time to start setting about getting to know them better. Sometimes I will test new areas to share by posting a few meme's that cover a particular topic. Then I sit back and watch to see how well received it is. Is it shared many times? Do people click like or even better yet, do they click the love button? Are people commenting on the post or is it silent? Tracking all of these factors is how you will discover what works for you and your customers.

TIP: Be sure to reply to their comments if you know what's good for you! The algorithms will see this as proof of engagement.

In an attempt to break down all my targeting campaigns for social media, I broke out a package of index cards. From there I wrote down each category and aspect of my business that I felt needed to be worked on. Problem cards included purses, shoes, jewelry, holiday trends, sweaters, winter coats, scarves, etc. Soon the floor was littered with cards and I felt overwhelmed. After all, with all the daily duties of a consignment shop, integrating social media just seemed like an additional burden. One that I simply didn't have time to tackle, or so I thought. After hiding my hideous pile of index cards and ignoring them for a few days, something hit me. I was scrolling through my Facebook personal feed and it dawned on me that I WAS ON SOCIAL MEDIA YET CLAIMED TO BE TOO BUSY FOR IT! Let that sink in. Instead of scrolling through various recipes, memes and posts about babies learning to crawl, I should be delivering amazing content on this platform that I already spend so much time on. That was the moment I vowed to devote time to planning out my social media content.

CHAPTER 35
SOCIAL MEDIA GAME PLAN

Right before my eyes our children are growing up. For some reason this hit me especially hard this past summer. It was while at a conference in San Antonio that I realized I needed to take a social media break. Now let's be clear, it's unrealistic to stop social media altogether, so a plan had to be made.

For the longest time I had considered planning out my posts, yet I never actually implemented it. In an attempt to take time off from social media, I decided to take the plunge. What happened next made me want to kick myself in the seat of the pants for dragging my feet for so long!

The first thing I did was start finding engaging posts to share with my readers. I was scheduling posts like a madwoman before I realized that there was no rhyme or reason to them. If you are going to schedule posts then you need to plan accordingly.

My first attempt to plan out social media went like most of my maiden voyages. I crashed and burned. Blindly scheduling posts for the future so that I was consistently sharing only backfired. As it turned out, on a few days I had several posts scheduled while other days you could hear crickets chirping. Turns out that planning social media content involves actual organization. Who knew?

Personally, I use a large wall calendar. Across the top I have listed above the days of the week a designated theme. Themes are handy especially if you know your followers and what they like to see. My themes surprisingly include much humor. My social content themes include fashion memes, consignment or shopping humor, pet funnies, vintage humorous memes, DIY projects for all different ages and holidays, repurpose and up-cycle projects, and family memes.

Once I designated each day of the week for the various themes, it made my job so much easier. Having the calendar allowed me to visually see which topics I needed to cover. This ensured that my social media was consistent with content. My goal was one post scheduled for each day. Using the calendar, I made a mark on each day of the month after I had successfully scheduled a post. This sounds so simplistic but it made a huge difference. It literally showed me at a glance which days of the month were completed and which days needed content. No longer was I struggling to look up what days were scheduled with what topics. Your method doesn't have to be fancy and cost a lot. It just needs to work for you.

Sticking to a regimen helps streamline the process of scheduling your posts. For example, when I go into the Facebook search bar I will enter the theme and then scroll through content to find what is acceptable for reposting. It has to be stated that when I refer to social media content I am reposting and sharing current Facebook content from other Facebook users. Facebook loves when you share its own content and this will gain you more momentum in visibility to your followers. Also, you don't want to be constantly only sharing content that revolves around selling your products. You have to hold relevancy with your followers or else why would they continue to follow you?

Always keep in mind that you do not want to offend anyone and the purpose of sharing social content is to keep it light hearted. Once I even did my own DIY after posting the directions. The task was easy enough, chalk paint an animal statue to make it more appealing. It was my opinion that my penguin and her baby were simply amazing! My bubble was burst when my husband took a look at my finished product and nearly spit his coffee everywhere. Imagine the before photo of an adorable momma penguin with her baby standing in front of her and then the after photo. A penguin chalk painted all one color, which turned the baby into what appeared as an appendage sticking out from a male penguin.

While the entire family and I giggled and snorted over this epic DIY failure, it compelled me to share my personal DIY. The post was a huge success. There was so much engagement in the form of comments and laughing emojis. So not only did the initial post do well, but the follow up post did even better. Despite the wild success of my posts, my family made me put away the chalk paint for good.

WHAT'S YOUR STATS?

Recently I've come to the realization that I'm seriously inept at social media follow through. I pride myself on promoting an event and creating hype around it. However when it comes to the actual event happening, I drop the ball. Every. Single. Time. This is difficult to admit but once an event takes place, I stop working it in the social media world. This is a gross misuse of a great opportunity to grow my customer base while reinforcing current engagement with my followers.

When we spend countless hours planning an event for whatever the purpose, we should keep in mind all the ways in which to further reach our audience. Consider all the people that showed an interest in the event. What if they saw LIVE coverage of the event? People having fun, getting great deals, whatever the event is. Those "interested" people might think twice the next time you host an event!

Now go a step further with follow up footage.

What if we posted a thank you post after the event, complete with photos? Again, this shows prospective guests what they missed as well as thanking and acknowledging those who did attend.

Be sure to set up the event for the best word of mouth by creating a photo booth or a selfie worthy station. It's the digital age! People love selfies and quick pics especially if it's a fun or worthwhile theme. The most important thing to remember is to brand your photo booth and make it easy for participants to tag you. Imagine the broad reach that is possible. Take advantage of all opportunities to let the world wide web know about your amazing store!

Let's discuss one final perk to follow through. Let's say the event was such an amazing success you decide to try it again down the road. By documenting the entire event you now have social proof and promotional footage for a future event. What better way to remind people WHY they should attend? Show them happy people taking advantage of an amazing event and make them realize they too need to participate. Remember that it also reminds previous participants why they should come again. It's a win/win situation. Unless of course the fire breathing troupe you hired to entertain set fire to a nearby car and the fire department was called to put it out. Then you might want to place that usb drive way back in your desk. Someday it will all be funny, I'm sure of it. Just not anytime soon.

In all seriousness, if you are identifying with this dilemma then please stop and pat yourself on the back. Acknowledging and accepting yet another facet to social sharing is all part of the fascinating world of social media success.

CHAPTER 36
A PICTURE IS WORTH A THOUSAND WORDS

This saying is so true and should always be in the back of your mind. Your sales depend on fabulous photos. You may not think this is true of your situation. Quality photos are not only for selling in an online auction. Photos are our best form of advertisement of all that our shop offers throughout all the forms of social media.

I cannot stress enough how important your photos are. Remember that the people viewing your photos can't examine the item as they would in person. What better way to give prospective consumers a peek into all that your store has to offer than to show them with a photo?

You don't need a degree in photography to take a well-lit and accurate photo. I'm just saying that with the right tools and equipment you can show your shoppers just how fabulous your item is. This is what generates sales, which is what makes you and your consignors money.

Having a photo that is bright and crisp is going to get that item sold faster than a dim photo. Personally, I struggle with photographing jewelry. Aside from the fact that I have chewed nails and would never cut it as a hand model, I struggle with the lighting and focusing on the intricate details of a quality Tiffany piece.

With little money you can create a home photography studio. A few years ago I traveled to Atlanta, Georgia to meet with Melissa Morales of Back By Popular Demand Consignment. She took the time to show me her impressive photo studio and all that it entailed. While Melissa showcases a higher level of merchandise, it was extremely helpful in creating my own photo space. The following are the essentials to creating your own photography studio at little to no cost.

My greatest piece of equipment for my store right now is an iPhone that I purchased for the sole benefit of the staff. This easily accessible phone allows all of them to snag quality photos with the most advanced filters and modes. Currently I'm crushing on the portrait mode of the iPhone. This makes everything slightly blurred in the background while the product stands out. Outstanding photos are a cinch with this feature.

Let's talk backdrops. Backdrops are an

important supply to have on hand. That is why I suggest that if you see material at a bargain price that looks like it has potential, buy it! You never know when it will come in handy as a photo backdrop. You can purchase backdrops online or you can pick out various bolts of fabric to complement your product. Another option is to purchase a canvas drop cloth from your local hardware store. They are generally quite large and allow you much versatility. Having an arsenal of various backings doesn't have to cost a lot. Once I used a furry white rug from my daughter's room to showcase a pair of high-end leather booties. Worked like a charm.

There are several variations of barn wood vinyl backdrops for sale. A few of them have made their way into my stash. Surprisingly, my rustic wooden counters remain the best sales tool for displaying items for the best picture. Go figure. The moral of this story is to start looking at your surroundings in a new light. Do you currently have a natural background that would be ideal for snapping pictures? Sometimes the best elements are right under our noses.

Contrast is another tip to keep in mind while taking pictures. What is the point of photographing a black sweater on a black backdrop? Not only will it camouflage the sweater, it will frustrate the person trying to view the sweater.

Outdoor lighting is the easiest way to obtain the

perfect lighting. Sometimes that is just out of the question and you must accommodate an indoor photo session. There are different lights available from Amazon that will fit your needs. Recently I heard a rave review from my good friend Suzy Pineda of Suzy's Consign & Resale shop in Indiana regarding the "ring light". It creates the most consistent glow to enhance your live videos as well as your photography sessions. Suzy does several Live Sales Videos on her store page and the lighting is always flawless.

Light Boxes are another excellent tool that don't require much money at all. A light box is simply a box with only one opening in which to photograph small items such as jewelry or shoes. We created one using a cardboard box. All we had to do was paper the inside of the box with plain white paper. Add some clamp on lights to the outer opening and voila! We had a well-lit space to capture those small items. If you go online, there are several tutorials that will help you build your own.

Mannequins are a secret weapon that help clothing come to life. When it comes to clothing, I find that if you can photograph the clothing on a mannequin or live model you will usually have better luck. Potential buyers prefer to see how the clothing will look when worn.

Do not be afraid to try different photography ideas. It will gain you experience, thereby making you a better photographer, which will therefore increase your sales. That's why I recommend photographing an item before beginning the posting process. This allows you to be creative and catch the true character of the item.

CHAPTER 37
SALES STRATEGIES FOR WORLD DOMINATION

There are lots of ways to lure shoppers in to your place of business. With all of the access to goods online, we must find a way to compete. There has to be a unique approach to our marketing strategies that provides the customer with an in-store experience that an online sale doesn't come close to achieving. The past few months I've diligently worked at trying to achieve just that. (My inspiration came from the resale guru, Kate Holmes of the www.tgtbt.com website). Kate issued a challenge to stop devaluing our merchandise by simply holding a percentage off sale. Easier said than done, I've tried all sorts of tactics. Keep in mind that everyone's situations are entirely different. If you are as stubborn as I am, and don't stop trying you will eventually figure out what speaks to your customers.

One of my maiden voyage trials was to host a weekly event called Margarita Mondays. It was supposed to be a joyous end to a dreaded Monday. Our shop would simply be providing small sized portions of Margaritas. After all, who doesn't love a Margarita especially after the first day back to work?

The icing on the cake was a free five-minute massage for everyone in attendance. There was a recent graduate from massage school who was hungry for clients. She was receptive to the idea of an opportunity to grow her customer base. Massages were going to be free and she would take the opportunity to hand out business cards.

The launch of Margarita Monday's was highly anticipated by our sales team. We would be hitting it out of the park! Guess what? It was an epic disaster and not very well received. We tried it for two full months and it just never took off. There weren't many in attendance and a few times I drank more than my fair share of Margarita samples. To this day I have a few bottles of Tequila stashed in the back office closet. It serves as an excellent reminder of the sobering fact that not all grand ideas work.

As an entrepreneur we must persevere and look at a failure as a learning tool. Once I let go of my ego, I came to the very important realization that

KIRSTY ROEFS

my particular market was not a fan of alcohol events. Lesson learned and the silver lining was that I had an arsenal of Margarita mix and tequila on hand in case of emergency.

With that information in mind, we launched a weekend event to start incorporating crafts for kids. We set out to purchase child friendly craft kits that would be practically maintenance free on our part. Easy peel and stick tissue paper crafts and coloring kits seemed to be a hit. Then my stinginess got the best of me and I ordered a kit of do-it-yourself sun-catchers that were on clearance. That should have been my first omen that it wasn't a good idea. You guessed it, first kid to use the paint squirt bottle, squirted it directly into his eye ball! Thankfully he survived with minimal burning and will probably possess an unhealthy craft-phobia for life.

Another valuable lesson learned. Keep it simple and be sure to host events that are safe for people of all ages. Anticipate the worst possible scenario and use that as a guide. From that experience we learned that safety must always be foremost on our mind.

We've had event fails, but we've also had huge successes. Everyone's heard of the trendy paint and sip events. Adults gather and sip wine and then with the help of an artist, they are guided with step-by-step instructions to create an artistic masterpiece. Our area was inundated with events such as this. Sierra Boice, my right hand woman and long time employee, introduced the idea of hosting a mommy and me event without the alcohol but rather with hot cocoa and snacks. Sometimes it is hard to carve out quality experiences with our children. We provided that creative experience in a part of our store. It takes a lot of work and organization but it allowed us to reach an even greater base of mothers in our area. Not only mothers but grandmothers were signing up for the events. They were drawn to the event and they couldn't help but shop while here.

I am most fortunate to have a creative and artsy genius such as Sierra. Is there someone in your area who would also be excited at the prospect of hosting such an event? Thinking outside the box is the key to beating the big box stores.

CHAPTER 38
BAG SALES

It's inevitable that not all your merchandise will sell. As cheap as I am, I have worked very hard at extracting every last penny out of items that I have invested time and energy into. We sort them, we tag them, we display them and we pull them for donation. That item has been handled several times and has cost me money to do so.

The first obvious concern is that I pay attention to why a particular item didn't sell. Was it priced incorrectly? Was it hideous and outdated with no business being on my sales floor? Was the item placed in the wrong location so that it didn't have a chance to sell? These are all things to consider when going through your unsold items. Once I've ascertained why it didn't sell, I need to move those items to make room for items that will sell.

For a long time I would pull and immediately donate them to local charities. As the years went by I realized that I wanted to extract more money out of these items. It took some doing but my husband built a caged locker of sorts in the back part of our store's basement. It would house the unsold items in plain garbage bags. The first year we attempted this, we were a disaster. Nothing was labeled and it was basically a free for all. To my pleasant surprise, people were extremely receptive to the bag sale idea and it's grown in popularity over the years. People come from miles around to this event. We hold them twice a year, once in spring and then again in the fall. We've come a long way with our bag sale procedures and that is proven by the steady climb of sales revenue it generates.

Our first sale was busy and it taught us to be more organized. As we conquered this, the sales grew larger and before we knew it, we had to move the sale out of the store altogether as there were so many people in attendance that it was unsafe. Imagine a wall-to-wall confined space of bodies. It was time to move this huge event to the great outdoors.

We enclosed our front yard with a picket fence not only to contain our children but to also keep the bag sales easily manageable. There was one point of entry on sales day. My husband George had to assume the host role of these sales as my nerves couldn't handle the large crowd of shoppers. He sells the bags to shoppers as they enter the gate to the yard where all items are organized by piles. People are encouraged to stuff their bags all they want. After all, the more they haul away means the less we have to bag up at the end of the day.

The first item of business was to label all the garbage bags with the contents. We broke down our clothing categories into men's, boy's, baby, girl's, women's S, M, L, XL and plus. By labeling these bags by department it made it easier once sale day arrived. Instead of a monstrous pile of clothing with a mix of everything, we were able to easily sort the sizes and genders based on the labels on the outside of bags. Through an online print service we were able to make yard signs to help organize the event. A sign was placed near each pile that clearly stated the gender and size. This helped save people much time and energy sorting through massive piles. It also allowed the space to be broken up and allow foot traffic to flow throughout the sale's set up.

We only run the sale for one day. After the sale is over, we bag up and donate the leftover items. They have had every opportunity to be picked over and we want to keep things moving.

One thing to keep in mind is that when you host a special sale like this, people want you to stick to your hours. A few years ago we were distressed as we woke on bag sale day to a torrential rain and lightening storm. Despite the horrible conditions, people were forming a line an hour before we were scheduled to open. A mere 10 minutes prior to the sale time, we decided to open up so that the people could at least be under the tents. People that arrived at 10 am and discovered the sale underway were furious. Upon reflection, I'm grateful lightening didn't strike any shoppers and most of all the clothing was sold. It was a wet and miserable day, yet the appeal of the bag sale was so great that it didn't discourage many. It was one of the best bag sale day figures on record.

These sales are an excellent draw to our shop. Not only do we move much merchandise that we would have otherwise donated, but we were able to squeeze a few more dollars out of it. Ironically, after the shoppers score their bag sale treasures they come into the store and shop. It's one of our more lucrative sales days. The entire day is exhausting but well worth it. If you can figure out how to store this overflow of merchandise, I highly recommend it.

CHAPTER 39
EVENTS

Events take some forethought and planning. The simpler you keep them, the easier they are to accomplish. If you have an event bomb, do not fear. Have a heart and look to figuring out what does work for your audience. Consequently, if you have an event that does extremely well or is well received, be sure to track that and record it. Keeping track of these effective sales events could set you up for an easier sales year in the future. By organizing your events and reusing ideas, you are making life easier on yourself.

Free stuff is an excellent way to not only lure in your customers but to validate their doing business with you. Who doesn't love to receive gifts? One of my favorite things to do is stalk wholesale sites for deals (except when it's squeeze bottles of paint).

Pinterest is another obsession and I try to make my time spent on there worthwhile. Forever searching for unique ways to thank my customers and consignors, I've gotten a few proven ideas.

HOLIDAYS

Have you ever been driving along and you hear of some kooky holiday on the radio? For years I had been laughing over particular days. Then I started looking ahead to upcoming months and what unique holidays they offered. Turn them into an in-store event of some sort. Promote it, and actually create a Facebook Event so people can RSVP.

There are holiday calendars devoted to these bizarre and quirky holidays. There's even an email notifications alert you can sign up for. It is my opinion to look at a year at a glance and plan these events out. You can save much money by planning ahead for these special events.

Let me share a few of my favorite, most adaptable holidays with you.

EMMA NUTT DAY

Emma Nutt day is one of my favorites because I make it all about me! Honestly, I don't really but I am the one with the costume. With some simple accessories and Pinterest assistance, I was able to easily dress the part of Emma Nutt. If you aren't aware of who she is, let me tell you. Emma was the world's first female telephone operator in Boston, Massachusetts. She accomplished this feat on September 1, 1878. To honor a woman who helped bring me my current freedom to conduct business and have all the same rights as a man, I am glad to keep her name and her spirit alive. All we did for this event was have me dressed as Emma and engage with customers about who I was portraying. Some customers even asked to be photographed with me. It was an experience.

Is there a local historical figure in your community you could portray? Possibly do it in conjunction with a local historical celebration and voila! You are suddenly standing out as a community member and showing your preservation of history as well as furthering your store's brand.

NATIONAL FORTUNE COOKIE DAY

Another great event that people enjoyed was National Fortune Cookie Day. For $17, I ordered 200 fortune cookies from Amazon. We promoted the event and offered free fortune cookies in celebration of the day. It doesn't get any easier than that! The only glitch was the crabby woman who kept stuffing her pockets with the FREE fortune cookies. Before you wonder if she was hungry and less fortunate, don't. My only concern was that she might have crushed up the dozen fortune cookies she swiped as she hopped into her new sleek Cadillac coupe. This woman was not down on her luck. She was just a real crab with a wild streak of snatching free cookies. Let's just chalk this experience up to the cost of doing business. Aside from the cookie snatcher, several people were excited to receive a free fortune cookie and couldn't wait to read their fortunes.

FLAG DAY PARADE FLOAT

My local hometown of Unadilla has several claims to fame. Not only are we the home to the Boy Scouts of America's Troop #1 but we also have held the longest continuously running Flag Day parade in the nation. This is a big deal for us and the streets are packed with people who come out to view this big parade. This is one of my shop's most favorite events as we all work together to come up with unique and patriotic themes each year. Costumes and swag are thought out months in advance. All staff and my family dress up and decorate the float. It's a blast and people are always wondering what we will come up with from year to year. Just as important as the debut of our float is the swag that we throw to the crowd. One year we threw frisbees with our logo on them. A sticker made from address labels that we printed was stuck to the inside of the frisbee with a coupon to our shop. Another year we had a few staff walk in costume alongside the float to hand out patriotic red, white and blue pinwheels to the crowd. Of course, there was a business card taped to the stem. Sticking with the candy that people love to catch from a float, we recently threw lollipops into the crowd with a small sticker attached with our logo on them.

BLACK FRIDAY

Black Friday is a shopping phenomenon that everyone should embrace. Some local businesses opt out of this event, which I will never understand. Black Friday doesn't only pertain to big box stores, but small businesses as well. Our Black Friday sales days are typically a banner day. If you don't put yourself out there, you are definitely not going to score big. All of the staff dressed in black for Black Friday and we sent out notices the night before for a FREE GIFT to all the people who shopped with us that day. The gifts were small zip lock jewelry bags with our logo and the words, "Holiday Survival Kit." Inside were tic-tac samples, aspirin samples and hand sanitizer wipes. They were well received by the public and we plan on doing the same next year.

SMALL BUSINESS SATURDAY

PLAID-urday was something that worked extremely well for us. While most shops ran with the Small Business Saturday theme, we upped our game. We all dressed in plaid and held a 50% off sale for anything with plaid on it. When customers entered they were greeted with a gift. A small Christmas tree tag we punched from a craft stamp onto plaid craft paper. Then we had punched two tiny holes in the tree so that we could fasten faux diamond posts.

I purchased these wholesale and they didn't cost much at all. However, repackaged, they looked quite stunning and tied in perfectly with our plaid theme. People of all ages seemed excited for the free gift. Men that didn't have holes for earrings were offered a free piercing by myself. They all refused once they realized I was going to use my hole punch. Not very adventurous of them but nonetheless it was available should they not want to feel excluded. Several plaid pieces sold that day and people chuckled over our Plaid-urday campaign. That's a win in my book.

MARKETING IDEA:

Do your own version of Elf on the Shelf showcasing a stylish "elf" appearing in the various departments of your store. Promote this via social media and with in store signage. What antics would your store elf get into?

CONTEST IDEA:

Guess how many are in a jar... Customers enter by writing their guess on their business card! Closest guess WINS the jar and its contents. This is an easy way to build hype on your social media and in-store. It also doesn't have to cost a small fortune.

CHAPTER 40
COMMUNITY

A few local businesses banned together to create an event to draw awareness to all our small village had to offer. We wanted to be a destination for people in surrounding areas. The local hardware store, the coffee shop and a few consignment shops all participated in hosting a coffee crawl.

Each business hosted a particular flavor of coffee. Attendees would each get a business card (which we printed very economically with a coupon from Vistaprint) and at each business they would get a free cup of coffee. They would also get a unique hole punch from each location. Their goal was to obtain a hole punch from each location, completing their card.

The event was extremely well received by the public and was well attended. As an extra special touch, my family made several dozen chocolate covered candy cane spoons, which we wrapped in cellophane and tied with curling ribbon. We then attached a coupon to the ribbon to reinforce our store brand and send them home with a tangible reminder to come back and shop again. It was our unique approach, an alternative to the usual alcohol crawl, which made people respond so well. Children were in tow and we all had a banner sales day. We are looking to make this a yearly event to continue the momentum.

With the success of the coffee crawl, we rallied again for St. Patrick's Day. We hosted a scavenger hunt throughout the village with several businesses participating. We created a game plan that each business would have a particular St. Patrick's object. These included a golden teapot, shamrock, leprechaun, rainbow, and a pot of gold. Each business was responsible for supplying the scavenger item in their store. Our store was to hide a shamrock. Thinking I would make it fun and easy, I asked my neighbor John, who is a talented artist to construct and paint a four-foot shamrock. It was so well done and life like. For some bizarre reason however, people were struggling to find it even though it was in plain sight. Everyone who came in to my shop that day was given a lucky shamrock. All this consisted of was a shamrock cutout with a scratch off coupon for a later date in time. Who doesn't love scratch-offs? Especially when they're free.

Local community events are achievable. If you create an event, not everyone will be willing to jump on board at first. However, upon the success be forewarned that many businesses will change

147

their tune and want in on the next one. With a little research and knowledge of local events, see how you could participate and get on board with them. Some suggestions as to where to look include your local chamber of commerce, rotary, school events, and charity drives. After all, the more the merrier.

CHAPTER 41
CROSS PROMOTIONAL SALES EVENTS

Take a moment and think about all the people you currently know who sell using a multi level marketing business. These sorts of businesses range from cosmetics to kitchenware. If you know of a particularly motivated individual, I would suggest working together on an event that would mutually benefit both of you. Allowing them to set up in your shop for a special event or on a particular day will allow you to not only help out a fellow entrepreneur, but also expose their clientele to your business brand. Cross promotion is invaluable and when done correctly, could help significantly increase your customer base.

Think larger yet and consider all the other types of entrepreneurs you are acquainted with.

One of my most popular events is with a talented local photographer, Sierra Boice. She is the owner of Sierra Rain Photography and she is a motivated and charismatic entrepreneur. Her enthusiasm to help capture memories and stages of a family's life are what drives her business. During various times of the year, she will set up mini photography sessions in the store. Quite often this helps to introduce consignment to an array of new families that might not be familiar with our store. It puts House of Consignment on the map as a destination while helping a fellow business minded woman achieve her dreams. A total win/win situation. Crucial to success is that there be a clear line of communication and all details regarding any monetary exchange is determined prior to the event.

Remember that friend of mine who suggested I close my shop because I was whining so much? Miranda Couse is the mastermind behind the wildly successful baking blog *Cookie Dough and Oven Mitt*. Miranda and my relationship is forged together with sugar and icing as I am her personal taste tester. In October 2017, Miranda released her first cookbook, *The Easy Homemade Cookie Cookbook*. It is with great pleasure that I am able to brag that I taste tested each and every sweet treat in that book! An additional 15 pounds of weight to my waistline will prove it!

With the anticipation of her cookbook release, we began planning a book signing in our shop. She had a beautiful sampling of her cookies and was also signing her cookbook for all who purchased one. It was a fantastic turnout and helped locals realize all that our local community had to offer. That two-hour evening event helped to move merchandise, demonstrate our support of local entrepreneurs and helped Miranda gain exposure and sales. With minimal effort and low cost, we were able to create an event that showed locals we were an event hotspot.

A few years ago we had new neighbors move in. It was nice to see a vacant house being lived in again. It wasn't until later that it came to light that a bestselling author had moved in. Cat Johnson is someone whom I enthusiastically call my friend. She is a powerhouse to be acquainted with and I feel as if we struck gold when she and her husband moved in. Hesitant to intrude yet so excited to have a romance writer in our small village, I asked her if she would be interested in attending our No Strings Attached Tampon party. She obliged us and was glad to bring several copies of her book in, which she autographed for fans. Not only did she give us that celebrity piece by simply partaking in our event, but she graciously donated a beautiful romance basket complete with signed copies of some of her books! Her attendance was a huge asset in our efforts.

Is there a local entrepreneur whose business would coincide with yours in a favorable light? Invite them to join forces on an event and you'll both benefit!

PART 4
PROCEDURES & POLICIES

GETTING DOWN TO BUSINESS

While I would much rather chat about the wildly exciting stuff that consignment dreams are made of, we must tackle the mundane. Part of being a success in business is to have your procedures and policies as well as your pertinent forms in order. It's not the glamorous aspect of business, however it is essential. So let's get down to business!

CHAPTER 42
THE CONSIGNMENT CONTRACT

Here is a copy of my brick and mortar consignment contract. The more examples you locate to review, the better you will be able to determine which policies and terms of service you would like to incorporate into your own contract.

House of Consignment

214 Main St. Unadilla, NY 13849

www.houseofconsignmentNY.com

(607)369-2827

Account #_____

We're pleased that you want to consign with us. We strive to keep the consignment process easy:

When you bring your items in to consign, we will select what we feel our customers will buy. Sometimes there will be items we cannot sell. Please understand that our customers' preferences must be our guideline.

Once an item is consigned, it will pass through several sets of hands before it hits the sales floor. Sometimes we may discover an item flaw after acceptance. Any items not meeting our standards may be donated after original pre-sort. House of Consignment reserves the right to place items on the sales floor at our discretion.

We base prices on supply and demand. We will price it at the best possible prices for you as we are splitting it 60/40. In addition to the selling price there will be a nominal buyers fee. This small fee is to cover credit card costs and the costs of pricing items. Please stop in during our business hours to pick up money owed to your account. We are open daily 10am – 6pm.

We will display your items for 60 days. During that 60 day consignment period, items may be subject to periodic sales which will result in a lower selling price. After 60 days, unsold items become the property of the House of Consignment. Unsold items will not be pulled for consignor pickup. Unsold items will be repurposed to aid our various charitable causes. We pledge to do our best to safeguard your items, but we are not responsible for damaged or lost items.

House of Consignment reserves the right to make decisions to change our policies and/or provisions in this contract with regard to future changes that might occur.

We look forward to a long and mutually profitable association with you. After all, we couldn't do it without you, our partner in consignment!

I have read the above consignment information and hereby approve this agreement.

Signed

Date

Printed Name

Phone

Address

Email

CHAPTER 43
SOFTWARE

When the first resale shop was born many years ago, there was a massive amount of tedious paperwork involved. There were no computers to keep your many consignors' and customers' information easily stored in a database.

In the beginning, I'll admit it crossed my mind to handle it all by hand. The thought of investing a large sum of money on software seemed unrealistic. Nowadays, I feel it is an absolute necessity. Software is most definitely a cost of doing business in this modern world.

Let's begin with the fact that understanding how to enter tags under a consignors' account number and looking up how much money you owe a particular consignor is only a tiny part of your software. These programs are amazing and have so many features that allow you to look realistically at your business. The most valuable resources are at your disposal on a daily basis. It is very beneficial to actually read your manual. Getting to understand all the different reports will help you grow your business more than anything else.

Prior to attending my first NARTS (National Association of Resale Professionals www.narts.com) conference, I was guilty of not even having the slightest idea of how to access all of my software's potential. It wasn't that I was intellectually unable (not entirely anyway). It was because I had no time. The day-to-day duties and never ending problems that arise didn't leave me with a lot of hours to allocate to "paperwork". What a misguided notion that was.

It is imperative that you make time to review your sales reports. Even more important is that you review your non-sales reports. In the back of my mind it was bothering me that my maternity section was always overflowing and just not getting shopped. Trying different locations, different displays, nothing worked to get that department off the ground and making me money.

While overhearing a conversation at my first NARTS conference, I discovered that I could run a "slowest selling category" report. What I discovered was that I was not moving maternity clothing at all! It was wasting energy and payroll to sort them, tag them and occupy space on the sales floor unnecessarily. It was basically costing me money to NOT sell maternity clothes. My initial reaction was to feel like an utter fool. Honestly, this is my go to response for most situations. After eliminating the maternity clothing it dawned on me. This was a learning lesson that forced me to grow. It made my business more profitable and was a stepping stone for a better use of my resale space. The information was there all along, I just hadn't known how to access it. That lesson catapulted me into an intense obsession with the reports function of my software.

If you are feeling queasy at this point of the book, STOP! Keep in mind that I had my software for 12 years before I accessed the reports. Now that should give you some perspective and some encouragement as well. Start small but please be sure to start just the same.

Most software systems allow you to track your customers as well as your consignors. In the point of sale module (for those of you who aren't sure, point of sale is your cash register for ringing up sales at checkout) you quite often have the option of selecting or inputting a customer's information. This is an excellent method to gather their information. Name, address, phone number and even birthday. You offer them the incentive of getting a birthday month coupon if they resist. Most won't want to tell you their birth year, so don't put too much stock in that or you will get skewed information. After all, I've been 39 for the past 5 years! Keep in mind that if you gather only consignor information, you are losing out on a larger segment of your sales base. Some software companies offer the option to keep track of sales in the form of a loyalty program.

There are many different options available with having a quality software program at your fingertips. Above all else, be sure to feel absolutely comfortable with the software you decide on. Many reputable consignment software companies will have the option of a sample program. This is something that I cannot stress the importance of enough. Think of it like this, you will hopefully be using this software system for a very long time. The software is the heart of your business. Therefore it is absolutely crucial to make sure you are ready to enter into a long-term relationship with one particular software before purchasing it impulsively.

CHAPTER 44
STORE LOCATION

Location is an important factor when setting up your store for success. Before you jump at the first opportunity it is important to take the time to evaluate your needs. Parking is a necessity that should not be overlooked. This applies to potential shoppers being able to find a parking spot and also to your consignors who are supplying your sales inventory. Consignors have already taken the time to sort and gather their unwanted items. Don't add to their workload by making the trek into your shop unbearable. If it's difficult to cart their belongings in to you, they will be turned off and could decide to donate rather than struggle.

The convenience we offer is key to repeat business with consignors. This also applies to our shoppers. Make accessibility to your shop easy with having ample parking as well as a safe location in which to enter.

Is the potential location in a safe neighborhood? What kind of access does your shop have? Have you taken the time to clearly define what types of inventory you plan on carrying? Will you need a large door for furniture? Will you need an open floor plan to accommodate large pieces of furniture? Taking the time to think through your business plan is absolutely necessary. Even after you have your business plan all laid out, things will evolve after being in business. Don't let that discourage you though. Once you get a feel for your business and what works, change just means growth.

CHAPTER 45
STORE HOURS

Shortly after opening my brick and mortar store, I had to close early one Saturday. My youngest daughter decided to make her arrival into the world on what was shaping up to be a banner sales day. Despite my best efforts, I didn't quite make it in time and my husband wound up delivering baby Gracie. She was literally born into resale. We kept the store closed for two days, and then I opened up again on day three, back to work full-time. My daughter is now 15 years old, and to this day I have a customer who insists I'm always closed because of that two-day lapse. This story drives home the fact that consumers expect you to treat your business in a professional manner. Unless you're going into labor, I suggest that you take seriously your posted hours and stick to them. You don't want to get the reputation for being unreliable. One thing I pride myself on is that we are open when we say we are open.

As the store grew, it became evident that I needed to make it more accessible to my customers and consignors. Once a consignor has gone to the trouble of collecting and transporting items to my store, they are eager to unload them. If my store isn't open when they arrive, they're likely to simply dispose of them rather than return at another time to consign them with me. Likewise, shoppers are thrilled not to have to wonder, "Is she open on Tuesdays (or weekends or evenings)?"

This was a total game-changer for my business and my bottom line. During the years in which my store hours were limited, my business generated income. We were afforded a decent living. With the implementation of the new hours, open daily from 10 am to 6 pm, our business exploded with growth. The ease at which shoppers and consignors were able to access us meant that our database was growing at a fast pace. This brought a stream of new faces through our doors. It also meant that sales drastically increased. Our availability to consumers had a direct impact on our sales figures. This afforded HOC to increase staff, which allowed us to reach further. Now we had the time to create more eye catching displays. It afforded me the time to allocate to working on my business as opposed to working *in* my business. As the owner, it gave me the time to focus on growing my business to the next level.

CHAPTER 46
KEEP YOUR EMAILS CLEAN

Sending carefully thought out emails to your customer and consignor base is something that should never be neglected. Having your customers' emails allow you direct access to them. This is invaluable and should not be overlooked. Start collecting emails today if you haven't already.

Collecting the emails and creating a database is only the beginning. When was the last time you took a close look at your email contacts list? There are so many things we are responsible for and I rarely give it a thought. Recently it came to my attention that email service providers calculate your bill based on the size of your mailing list. It does not matter if they are valid or not. Ultimately, it is our responsibility to manage those contacts.

For me, I wasn't even aware of how many of

my email contacts were actually no longer valid. Imagine my dismay when I realized that I was being charged for over 600 emails that were of no use to me!

It's super important to monitor this yourself. Go in to your account and review your contacts list. If a contact states, "opt out" it means that the user no longer wishes to receive your emails. If a contact states, "bounce" then it means the user's mailbox is full or it is no longer in use. In some cases, a "bounce" could signal an email address that was entered incorrectly. Example:Kirsty@gmall.com when it should have been entered as Kirsty@gmail.com. Sometimes this is a simple fix but more often it is an old and ineffective email address.

Clear out those emails and breathe easy knowing that you are keeping on top of your charges.

CHAPTER 47
STAFF:
HOW TO GET GOOD HELP

There comes a time with almost any business when you must take on help in order to thrive. I resisted hiring with every ounce of my being. When I started my brick and mortar store, I was pregnant, had one feisty toddler and two small elementary sons who were wild as could be. Not ideal conditions to be starting a new business, but I was always one for doing things my own way. One thing I knew about myself was my complete inability to handle confrontation. Being the "boss" was something I feared. If I had it to do over again, I would have invested in some management courses and learned some skills for handling staff.

One of the toughest characteristics to determine in an interview is the potential staffer's level of "nice." If you have been out in public and encountered a particularly nasty employee while shopping, you know exactly what I mean. It's clear that during that person's interview they weren't snarling or proclaiming how awful it is to deal with customers. No employer in their right mind would hire someone with that attitude. Horrible employees know instinctively how much to show during an interview. Being able to identify this trait is hard for me, and probably for almost everyone. More difficult is the prospect of training such a person in how to be nice.

It is my opinion that each person interviewed deserves a response. In my arsenal of saved files is a standard email that I send out upon determining who won't make the cut. This saves time and gives the person closure.

From: Kirsty L. Roefs

Subject: Sales Associate Position

To:

Dear _____,

Thank you for applying for the sales associate position with House of Consignment. We appreciate your interest in our organization.

We received many applications for the position, and the hiring process has been a very competitive one. Although we were impressed with your qualifications, we have decided not to move your application forward. However, we greatly appreciate your interest in working with us and wish you the best of luck with your job search.

Sincerely,

Kirsty L. Roefs

Owner

CHAPTER 48
COMMUNICATION
AND EXPECTATIONS

Be completely honest with yourself. Are you a good communicator? When you think of communication, remember that it's a two-way process. Each party must understand the other. There have been times when I thought I was being very explicit with my directions, only to discover that my employee had no idea what they were supposed to be doing. If you want to be successful as an employer, make sure each individual employee understands your directions. Open dialogue is essential to ensuring that you are accurately conveying your thoughts. Encourage your employees to ask questions until they are sure they understand you. Effective communication involves both parties exchanging and sharing ideas and information.

Before you skim over this section because you feel you are already an articulate communicator, let me share a lesson that my three-year old niece taught me. While my kids and their cousins were playing, I watched as Gracie stood behind my niece Rachel and said, "Let's play trust fall!" Rachel had no idea what that was so Gracie explained that Rachel needed to just fall, and Gracie would catch her. In horror I watched as poor Rachel followed the directions and proceeded to fall face forward toward the floor.

Thankfully Gracie was agile and fast enough to snatch her backward. After a few heart pounding moments and reflection, it hit me that there was a very real lesson in this experience. Rachel was, for all intents and purposes, just like any employee. While Gracie thought she was giving clear directions, she had left out a valuable piece of information, which set Rachel up for failure. It is my advice that whenever you dole out responsibilities, task lists, etc., that you ensure that the instructions are clear cut and very detailed so as to avoid any misunderstanding. When in doubt, ask if your employee understands the directions.

Clear expectations are imperative for employee growth. One way in which to clarify your expectations for your employees is to have an employee manual in place. Going over this manual upon hiring them is crucial so that there are no misconceptions. To further enforce these conditions and employee accountability, I have set the last page of the manual as a page in which both I and the employee sign and date it. This drives home the importance of the document. It also sets conditions forth so if they become non-compliant, you have documentation to fall back on.

Please feel free to use my HOC employee packet as a guide for creating your own.

House of Consignment New Employee Packet

Mission: To be known as the leader in the consignment industry in the tri town area.

Mission: House of Consignment is committed to positively reflecting the resale industry by holding high standards for customer satisfaction, employee retention, business development, charitable giving, responsible recycling, and most of all, integrity in all that we do.

Core Values:

- Be honest
- Be respectful
- Be helpful
- Be on time
- Be generous

Re-Sale Associate Overview:

The re-sale associate is an entry level position with the possibility to be promoted within the company. The job functions are fundamental to the daily operations of the store and include customer service, merchandise processing, and facilities maintenance.

Job Description:

The re-sale associate must be a self-motivated individual with a friendly, upbeat attitude. Positive communication between management, team members, and customers is to be expected at all times. The re-sale associate has to have flexibility with scheduling and have weekend availability. Company core values are to be memorized and implemented in the day to day operations of the business.

Requirements:

- Love of the re-sale industry.
- Knowledge of clothing labels or the desire to learn.
- Knowledge of current fashion trends and styles.
- Superior people skills including the ability to build relationships with customers through verbal communication.
- Must be friendly, helpful, generous, punctual, and polite.
- Must be an industrious self-starter with the ability to efficiently complete individual tasks and projects.
- Must be a team player with an energetic spirit.
- Superior organizational skills.
- Must be able to stand for long periods of time and carry up to 25 pounds of weight.
- Have a basic understanding of simple math.
- Ability to learn our software program - Liberty.
- Ability to work around dust allergens.
- Scheduling Requirements:
- Employees must be willing and able to work

weekends, evenings and days before and after major holidays, especially the week of Thanksgiving.

- Employees must be available to work the week of the NARTS conference to ensure adequate staffing while owner attends. There are other critical weeks that are "black-out dates" for time off due to staffing needs. These will be posted as they arise.

- The store will be closed for 1 week in July and 1 week between Christmas and New Year's. This is an unpaid time off.

Duties and Responsibilities:

Customer Service

- Memorization and utilization of all customer service communication scripts. Must be able to communicate in an outgoing, confident, friendly, and helpful manner. Must greet each customer as they walk through the door.

- Use POS with confidence to ring up sales, as well as understand how to correctly ring up discounts and coupons.

- Memorize store policies to be able to answer any customer questions regarding the consignment process.

- Be familiar with the store layout and inventory. Be able to direct customers to what they are looking for.

- Assist customers with their purchases if you see them over loaded with items. Offer to make piles or offer them a basket so that they continue to shop. Also, show them to a dressing room should they want to try on clothing.
- Defer to management when a customer issue arises.
- Merchandise Processing
- Place merchandise in the correct place on the sales floor throughout the day.
- Ticket, secure, and hang correctly any merchandise that needs to be processed.
- Understand the markdown process and be able to complete markdowns correctly.
- Assist in creating well organized, eye catching displays to highlight merchandise.
- Pull expired merchandise to be sent to the appropriate location.
- Sort and price clothing when necessary.
- Facilities Maintenance
- Daily organizing of merchandise including sizing, colorizing, and straightening. Report to management when racks become difficult to shop.
- Report to management when store supplies are running low.

Disciplinary Action:

First offense - verbal warning

Second offense - written warning

Third offense – termination

Insubordination will not be tolerated.

Fire-able Offenses:

Under these circumstances below, normal disciplinary action procedure will not occur. Any employee who violates a rule under Fire-able offenses will immediately be terminated.

· Giving your 20% employee discount to a non-employee.

· Taking something out of the donate pile.

· Accepting merchandise to be consigned from a consignor as a gift.

· Buying something outright from a consignor for yourself, circumventing the consignment process for your own gain.

· Taking something home to try without paying for it. Everything that goes out the door must be paid for, period, no exceptions.

· Tardiness will not be tolerated. Be in at least 5 minutes before your scheduled shift. Call if you are detained for good reason.

· Falsifying your time card.

· Our job is to sell items, not hold them. You may not hold an item until it is reduced.

Employee Parking: All employees must park in the back driveway, reserving the front parking for customers.

Internet: The internet at House of Consignment is to be used for company purposes only. This includes research on products. Any other use must be approved by the manager.

Breaks: All breaks at House of Consignment are on the clock. If you wish to leave the store for lunch, you must clock out and inform the manager that you are leaving the premises.

Breaks are as follows:

· 4 hour shift or less, no break.· 4-6 hour shift, 10 minute break.· 6 hour shift or more, 20 minute break.

Cell phones: Cell phones must stay with employee's personal belongings. The use of a cell phone is not permitted during employee shifts unless used during an employee break.

It is our goal at House of Consignment to train all new employees to maximize their potential. Any employee who does not understand how to do something is encouraged to ask a manager to ensure all responsibilities are done efficiently and correctly.

Employee contact information:

Name Address

Phone #

E-mail

Birthday

I, _____ (print name), have read House of Consignments new employee packets and understand all its material. I also understand that failure to comply with any/all rules and regulations will result in disciplinary action and/or termination.

Signed

Date

CHAPTER 49
PUTTING OUT FIRES WITHOUT GETTING BURNED

Let's chat about dealing with staffing issues. I've been lucky enough to have several fabulous staff members who have given wholeheartedly to their position. They have been model employees and working with them has been a tremendous joy for me. Then there are the employees who have made me seriously doubt the integrity of the human race. Regardless of the experience, good or bad, if you can learn from it you're on the right track. Whether through cooperative learning or the simple act of putting your foot down, you are growing as a leader.

When I first embarked upon owning my own business I was fearful of employee confrontation. It wasn't my strong suit, and I'm still not fond of it.

However, it's an important part of my business. Without staff accountability, you can't improve your business, and without that there is no progress.

If I can stress one thing to you, it's that you must find the courage to speak your mind. Holding your thoughts and concerns in does your business no good. Communication is key to ensuring that your staff is properly equipped to represent your business and uphold the image you wish to project.

Once I realized that there was no easy way to achieve this other than buckling down and writing it all out and approaching it in a no-nonsense approach with the employee, life got a lot easier. By sharing with you some of my more horrendous tales from the employer perspective, I hope to impress upon you how important it is to tackle these problems head on and not let them fester. Also, it's imperative that you know when a situation is a losing battle, and you simply have to let an employee go. If you find yourself in this situation, it is vital that you document the event. Depending on state labor laws, having a termination record on file may be the thing that saves your business from having to pay unemployment costs. The following is the simple form that we use.

House of Consignment

214 Main Street Unadilla, NY 13849

Staff Disciplinary Report

Date

Employee Name:

Infraction Type:

Job Performance:

Policy/Conduct Core:

Disciplinary Action:

1st Written Notice:

2nd Written Notice:

Suspension:

Termination:

Deficiency/Infraction:

Actions to Correct Deficiency/Infraction:

Supervisor:

Employee:

In the past I've held onto employees way past their expiration date. This is not to say that I am a perfect boss, but it does mean that I pursued attempts to improve their job performance for so long that I was left with no option but to let them go. In one case I thought the world of the woman I hired, but in truth she was just a warm body with a poor work ethic who was just drawing a paycheck. She made no effort to improve. When I finally let her go, after stressing over my decision, she looked at me unfazed and actually said, "I had a feeling a few months ago that I wasn't doing a good job." That hit me harder than if she had exploded with anger. What an idiot I had been for allowing her to draw wages for so long as dead weight.

Now let's dive into the ugly side of being an employer: the point of no return, when you must follow through and get rid of an employee. DD isn't just my favorite coffee shop, it's also how I tackle the exit of an employee: Document and be Direct. The following are some examples of write-ups and some incident reports in which I had fellow staff document their eyewitness accounts. This is especially handy if the employee who is on the way out has stolen or committed some atrocious act, and you expect to have to defend yourself against an unemployment filing. Documenting is key if you want to stand a chance of winning an unemployment claim. Nothing burns me more than having to pay unemployment for a horrible employee who was terminated for good cause.

Since I'm a pushover, by the time I have to let an employee go the situation has usually gotten pretty bad.

In addition to documentation, I strongly recommend you be direct with the employee you are terminating. Have the termination paperwork in front of you and be matter of fact in your approach. Anything less than that and they will feel like they still have a chance of keeping their job. Don't let them weaken your resolve; if you have come to the point of firing, stick to your guns and follow through in a professional manner.

House of Consignment

Employee Incident Report

Name and role of person completing this form:

Kirsty Roefs Owner of House of Consignment

Signature of person completing this form:

Date:

INCIDENT

Date and time of incident:

Wednesday, April 20, 2016 at 4:30 pm

Name/s of person/s involved in the incident:

(employee's name)

Description of incident:

On the morning of Thursday, (date) I, (name) came to work to discover all the cash from the previous day laying in the cash register. It also was discovered that the credit card machine had not been batched out the night before. Standard protocol for (Employee in question's name) nightly routine was to: cash up the books, put the cash in the store safe and to batch out the credit card machine.

It was clear that (Employee's name) had simply left work without doing any of these things. She had left $ 780.04 in cash laying out. She hadn't even closed the cash drawer. She left $270.84 on the credit card machine, unsettled.

Witnesses:

(Employee who witnessed incident)

*Best to print the witness's name as well as have them sign.

CHAPTER 50
PUBLIC RELATIONS:
TOOT YOUR OWN HORN

Once while speaking to a large group of entrepreneurs, a woman stood up and asked how to get people to notice her community efforts. She was furious that she never received any recognition. While I sympathize with her, it is our responsibility to make sure there are no oversights. Writing a press release is so very important in order to let the world know what you are doing.

News worthy events include donating to locals in need, be it clothing or money. Did you collect items to donate? Did you recently expand your storefront? Are you preparing for a grand opening or a grand re-opening? Have you recently or plan to collaborate with a fellow business to accomplish a business goal? Is your business tied to a local upcoming holiday event? You want to make sure the press release is truly news. If you have received a new shipment of hats, that's not a press release. However, if you have a new shipment of hats and you plan on donating a portion of the sales to the local homeless, then that would be newsworthy.

There is a series of templates available online for writing a press release. The key ingredients to a good press release are to always include your store name and information. Be sure to come up with a headline that is not only catchy, but also sums up the press release content accurately. You will need to date the press release and be sure to provide a quote relating to the event being discussed. As for the body of the press release, you want to include any pertinent information regarding the event. Be sure to keep the who, what, when, where and why in mind when writing the body. If you are able to link it to the local community, be sure to add that. It's my normal practice to make the first sentence of the body a summarization of the events name, location and date.

The following is a press release that I submitted for Sock-Tober.

September 20, 2018

For Immediate Release:

Sock-Tober Event to Benefit Local Homeless Shelters

UNADILLA, NY– September 20, 2018 – House of Consignment, a local resale business in Unadilla is excited to be participating in a national event dubbed Sock-Tober.

The Association For Resale Innovation (ARI), a group of 34 consignment and resale store owners across the United States have banded together to hold a month-long "Sock-Tober" event. During the month of October, shoppers who purchase a pair of our affordable new socks may select a new pair to donate as well. Donation socks are available in men's, women's and children's styles and sizes.

ARI members believe in the importance of giving back to their communities in various ways and donating socks to the homeless is just our latest project to do so. The idea for donating a pair of socks for every pair purchased was developed at their last semi-annual conference held in Las Vegas in February.

Socks are a real need within the homeless community as they rarely are received. They defend against health issues, the upcoming cold weather and are sometimes called "white gold" among workers in social services. According to the website, The Joy of Sox, "sometimes socks can be more important than bringing people food because food is not hard to get but it seems to be harder and harder to get socks all the time."

Locally, House of Consignment is participating. Help this great cause at:

House of Consignment

214 Main Street, Unadilla NY 13849

www.houseofconsignmentNY.com

OPEN DAILY 10am - 6pm

Contact:

Kirsty Roefs, owner

House of Consignment

Phone (607)369-2827

hoc@stny.rr.com

Here is another press release example:

Hello! Here is the information pertaining to our upcoming Tampon FUNdraiser, was hoping to have this go along with our print ad.

Saturday, September 8 at 6pm the House of Consignment will be hosting a FUNdraiser for local women in need. HOC will be setting up a Halloween fest at the Unadilla Drive in. We will be playing the classic movies, *Hocus Pocus* followed by *Ghostbusters*. Cost of admittance is one box of tampons or pads per person, children included.

This is our third annual Tampon Drive and we are going all out with a witch's gift shop in which there will be Halloween and Hocus Pocus items for sale. In addition, there will be glitter tattoos and face painting. All profits benefit the tampon drive.

There is a real need for feminine hygiene products in our area. Females should not have to stress out over such need. We plan to stock local food pantries, and homeless shelters.

Be sure to email your press release to your local news outlets ASAP so that, if chosen, they may work it into their printing or posting. Quite often the press is looking for a good story to fill in small pieces of time. Why not let that be you? A simple press release could possibly lead to having a news crew coming out to do a quick story for the 5 o'clock news.

This happened to me recently and the momentum it gave me was immense. With only one hour to prepare before the news crew arrived, we hurried through cleaning the store. Of course on this particular morning, I had awoken late and threw on a hat and hoodie. My staff immediately shouted for me to run home and change. All was miraculously ready for when they arrived. It was over in a matter of minutes. They asked me a series of questions and I answered to the best of my ability. More so than the interview, we were all amazed at all we had accomplished in such little time. The simple fact that we could whip ourselves into shape that fast, made us realize our full potential. Sometimes you just have to kick it into high gear.

Aside from a press release, you should be documenting with photos on social media. It is important to tell your audience all that you do for your community. It reminds them that you are a small business making a big difference. This does not mean to constantly post and brag. A simple post showing the amount you collected or donated along with a catchy recap is all you need. We are always making donations and I feel that the people who contribute always appreciate seeing the end result. It ties them with your store and also encourages them to continue their relationship with you and your business.

CHAPTER 51
NEVER STOP LEARNING

Speaking to college students is one of my favorite experiences. Topics I've covered range from being a woman in business to the difficulties in business ownership. One of my recent speaking engagements with a group of local college students was enlightening, to say the least. At some point during the interactive presentation with a room full of IT and business students, the conversation evolved. The topic was social media and the impact it has with business owners. While I was explaining my difficulties in reaching out using social media, it occurred to me that I had a captive audience and they were all of a generation that I struggled with. Turning the tables, I opened the discussion and asked them to give me ideas.

My question to them was "how do I reach you?" Their response was nothing I expected. This generation is tech savvy yet their responses all directed me to a basic word of mouth form of advertising. They were insistent that they would rather find out about my business from a peer. This led to an entire conversation about brand ambassadors. Their suggestion to me was to cultivate a relationship with various people who would embody all the qualities of my shop.

Essentially, a brand ambassador is someone who promotes your business and receives certain perks in exchange. The brand ambassador is expected to help share your content and information on the various social media platforms in which they are involved. Their suggestion to me was to search out brand ambassadors on campus and offer them swag and discounts for spreading the word with their peers about my business. This had never occurred to me and yet it seemed so obvious. The biggest takeaway was that brand ambassadors want to feel special and they want to receive discounts and swag in exchange for promoting and referring my business. What better way to reach a specific target market than to utilize key people (in this case students) that are in amongst them? Not gonna lie, my mind was blown.

Most often they are rewarded with perks such as free gifts of items your store carries. For example, we carry the line of air fresheners called, Shelly's Smellies. If you haven't had the pleasure of smelling one, please go order one now! When Shelly releases a new scent, I could offer a free freshener to my brand ambassadors. In return, they would use the product and then promote it online and to their friends. This would not only drive customers to check out the Shelly's Smellies, but to see all that the House of Consignment has to offer.

Another perk of having brand ambassadors is that they are able to obtain feedback from customers and consignors and report back to you! This is excellent for figuring out which items are a smash success and which were not so well received. Use this feedback to further hone your business.

The takeaway from this experience was clearly that I needed to be a better listener, but more importantly I needed to go to the source for the best answers. After all, these students are our future customers and consignors and the sooner we figure out what motivates them, the better.

Another important learning tool in business is networking. I have made mention of several successful women in business throughout this book. We have met at various industry conferences. One of the best decisions I made was to attend a NARTS conference years ago. Not only did I further my education in the resale industry but I made friendships with others that understand my business. What an amazing asset, to be in contact with others that you can lean on during a difficult time. Chances are that they have experienced something similar to you. Being able to reach out and have someone to vent to or rejoice with is invaluable. Consider finding an organization to join that fits your business needs.

CHAPTER 52
HAPPY TRAILS:
IT WON'T BE EASY,
BUT IT WILL BE WORTH IT

There have been periods on this ride called entrepreneurship that made me wonder why I was in this line of business. Not every day as a business owner is as glamorous as an employee would think. There are days when I have to get out of bed and put on a smile while on the inside I'm wishing I was going off to a mundane job in which not much thought was required. We wear so many hats as an owner and some days are more difficult than others. Don't get me wrong. I love my store and I love the consignment industry. It's important to keep that in mind despite the down days.

Dealing with negative people is never easy. If you make the conscious choice to channel that distraught feeling into motivation to rise above the situation, you will be far ahead. It's not easy and I still have days when my insecurities are tested.

It is my hope that this book gives you some insight to all that you are capable of achieving in the environmentally hopeful world of consignment. With a lot of hard work and dedication you should be able to rely on this as a steady source of income within a short period of time. Nothing comes easy and starting a business is no different. When I first opened my brick and mortar store, House of Consignment, there were nights that I would put my children to bed and return to tagging. Weary nights and lack of sleep were not easy but it was imperative to ensure the success of my business. In a way, the House of Consignment was like having another child. The success of HOC depended on me much like the outcome of my children's lives depending on me ensuring they were parented. This meant that I had to make tough decisions that weren't always ideal but were necessary. Like parenthood, I wouldn't give up my store for all the tea in china. Maybe I should make that statement realistic. I wouldn't trade it for all the coffee in South America. After all, I'm really not a fan of tea.

.

CONTENTS

DEDICATION

This book is dedicated to my awesome husband, George.

Without him, none of this would have been possible. He has been my biggest supporter and my rock. Here's to many more years of living the dream. Kids. Chaos. The works!

ABOUT THE AUTHOR

Kirsty Roefs is the founder of the House of Consignment, and the author of the book Consignment from Home. A female entrepreneur, resale, social media and marketing guru, as well as a wife, mother and dog lover, she can usually be found planning her next charity event, rearranging the store, or making plans for world domination.

A resale professional since the year 2000, she has been the recipient of various honors including the Unadilla Chamber of Commerce 2018 Business of the Year, SUNY Delhi 2016 and 2017 Empowered Woman of the Year, and she was recognized by Job Corps of America, Days for Girls International and Family Resource Network for her community efforts.

She is an avid public speaker at resale and business conferences including NARTS (National Association of Resale Professionals) and ARI (Association for Resale Innovation).

She resides in upstate New York with her husband George and their 4 children.

Connect with Kirsty in the *Consignment from Home* Facebook Group.